THE ART OF
BUSINESS

D0706335

WITHDRAWN

of related interest

The Creative Arts in Dementia Care
Practical Person-Centred Approaches and Ideas
Jill Hayes
With Sarah Povey
Foreword by Shaun McNiff
ISBN 978 1 84905 056 2
eISBN 978 0 85700 251 8

Arts Therapies in Schools
Research and Practice
Edited by Vicky Karkou
ISBN 978 1 84310 633 3
eISBN 978 0 85700 209 9

Using Expressive Arts to Work with Mind, Body and Emotions
Theory and Practice
Mark Pearson and Helen Wilson
ISBN 978 1 84905 031 9
eISBN 978 0 85700 189 4

The Creative Arts in Palliative Care
Edited by Nigel Hartley and Malcolm Payne
ISBN 978 1 84310 591 6
eISBN 978 1 84642 802 9

THE ART OF BUSINESS

A Guide for Creative Arts Therapists Starting on a Path to Self-Employment

Emery Hurst Mikel

Foreword by Michael A. Franklin

Jessica Kingsley *Publishers*
London and Philadelphia

Consent forms have been provided for all case studies.

First published in 2013
by Jessica Kingsley Publishers
116 Pentonville Road
London N1 9JB, UK
and
400 Market Street, Suite 400
Philadelphia, PA 19106, USA

www.jkp.com

Copyright © Emery Hurst Mikel 2013
Foreword copyright © Michael A. Franklin 2013

Library of Congress Cataloging in Publication Data
Mikel, Emery Hurst.
  The art of business : a guide to self-employment for creative arts therapists / Emery Hurst Mikel ; foreword by Michael A. Franklin.
      pages cm
  Includes bibliographical references.
  ISBN 978-1-84905-950-3 (alk. paper)
  1. Psychotherapy--Practice. 2. Arts--Economic aspects. 3. Arts--Therapeutic use. 4. Arts management. I. Title.
  RC465.5.M552 2013
  616.89'1656--dc23
                          2012051508

British Library Cataloguing in Publication Data
A CIP catalogue record for this book is available from the British Library

ISBN 978 1 84905 950 3
eISBN 978 0 85700 772 8

Printed and bound in Great Britain

For my grandparents

Dr. John Ralph Emerson Hurst Jr. and Mrs. Jane Baldwin Goodrich Hurst for the love as their only granddaughter and for teaching me how to make my way in the world, help others, and cherish family and history.

Mrs. Amy Arminda Chambers Mikel and Mr. Russell Delbert Mikel Sr. for showing me the love that comes from a crazy family, the healing of gathering together, and the patience as well as other gifts that can come with Alzheimer's disease.

For my parents

Alison Hurst, who taught me how to love, to trust my instincts, and is always there for me in every way, every day of my life.

Russell Delbert Mikel Jr., who taught me that change is always possible and instilled in me my love of code cracking and problem solving.

For my brother

Jory Hurst Mikel, who taught me to treasure the small moments, how to teach, how to learn, and to value the differences in people.

For all the amazing people who work with seniors

For the families affected by Alzheimer's disease

And finally…

I wrote this book because of the elders in my life and everything they teach me on a daily basis. How to stay open and listen even in uncertainty and how understanding, patience, and caring surpass so much.

CONTENTS

FOREWORD

Years ago I went to a talk and performance by John Cage, the 20th century avant-garde composer. During a segment of his presentation, he spoke about unemployment as self-employment, referencing the vast freedom to be found in finding one's authentic vocational path. I was reminded of Cage's point when reading Emery Mikel's book on self-employment for expressive therapists. Why? All too often people have rigid ideas when it comes to their career paths. In fact, when some people attempt to think outside of the box, especially when it comes to employment, they end up creating a new one. For example, expressive therapists often want to choose private practice as their occupational goal, thinking this to be the most viable, lucrative option. Few people, even seasoned therapists, venture into contract work as a feasible choice.

In this thoughtful book, Emery Mikel imagines beyond limiting career options by combining convergent and divergent creative thinking to conceive this inventive, yet practical manual for self-employment. By teasing apart and combing through the similarities and differences inherent in private practice and contract relationships, Mikel lays the groundwork for thinking about this alternative employment option. Knowing that this choice will be daunting for many, Mikel makes the process accessible—even fun—by adding art-based exercises to creatively problem solve the likely obstacles that will surface. From her years of experience, she presupposes that barriers do exist and that they will surface, and explains how to maintain a contemplative point of view while negotiating unforeseen complications. Furthermore, Mikel looks into the shadows, corners, and even in the cracks of various possible scenarios, anticipating all sorts of problems and solutions.

She has learned to cast her skills wide and develop strategies for any number of questions needing resolution.

In these challenging economic times, expressive therapists deserve to be prepared for diverse vocational opportunities. In order to achieve this goal, sound business strategies are needed. This book presents a sensible foundation for skillfully joining personal creativity, vocational aspirations, and solution-focused strategies for contract work. We are really at our best when we surpass our self-imposed barriers...it is time to think outside of the box, and through the example of contract work, bring our profession to the diverse waiting public ready to benefit from the expressive therapies.

Michael A. Franklin, Ph.D., ATR-BC
Professor and Coordinator, Graduate Art Therapy Program
Naropa University, Boulder, Colorado

ACKNOWLEDGMENTS

Thank you and immeasurable gratitude to:

Carol Thayer Cox who was there at the beginning of this adventure with unwavering support and whose excitement and encouragement helped launch me into contract work. Rebecca Wilkinson, who journeyed with me, drawing mandalas side by side, and kept me looking forward even when we weren't sure where the path would lead. Lisa Garlock for bringing me into the GW community and allowing me to inspire her students. Michael Franklin for his contribution to this work, recognizing the value of the spaces between my words and for cherishing Mr. Bear. Sue Wallingford for nurturing and helping me express the complex emotions that come when working with the elderly and people with Alzheimer's disease. Merryl Roathus for understanding and helping me face my challenges with gentleness. The late Bernie Merak for just letting me go and trusting I would finish my dinosaur in time. Paula Randazzo for giving me the freedom and confidence to run groups while staying in the moment and trusting my instincts. Duane Mullner and my amazing counseling class for carrying me through the hard times and beating the hell out of those pillows when I couldn't do it myself. Dottie Oatman for her understanding, guidance, and creating a space for Fred and Lotus to live in her studio.

Michael Schatz for the many adventures we went on together and for his love and support as I worked through graduate school and figured out how to do the work that I love.

Jessica Kingsley Publishers. In particular, Lisa Clark for seeing the possibilities in my manuscript and guiding me through the process, along with Lucy Buckroyd, Victoria Nicholas, Tony Schiavo, and everyone else who put their time and effort towards this book becoming a reality.

Everyone who supported this adventure through editing, proofreading, contributing, or just being there: Firouz "Fizzy" Ardalan, Teresa Barrett, Donna Newman-Bluestein, Gioia Chilton, Audrey Evans, Angela Tatum Fairfax, Anna Ford, Faith Halverson-Ramos, Catherine Harris, Russ Kaplan, Crista Kostenko, Sara Miller,

Natalie Mullis, Sami Osman, Mira Reisberg, Bev Therkelsen, Sarah Thompson, Gayle Torres, and many others.

Interns Genevieve Camp and Katryn "Kitty" Ellis for their uniqueness, inspiring questions, and engaging conversations.

Lung Chuan Fa, my entire Kung Fu family, and especially Shifu Doug Moffat, for always being there and pushing me to reach my full potential in every way possible: polar dips, black sash testing, hanging off rocky ledges. A special thank you to Leah Baldo, Jennifer Fenton, and Nathan Toxopeus for their friendship, guidance, and support. Susi and Damon Metz for bringing me into their family and letting me play with the two cutest kids in the world whenever I needed to cuddle.

Naropa classmates: Katie Dischler-Drobney for fire dancing; Agnieszka Gorska for always being there; Lynn Gillis for her love and support; Marguax Laughlin for her patience and understanding; Cherilyn Boswell for caring and inspiration; Sibel Ozer for her insight and wisdom; Chelsea Leitner for her creativity and the purple rabbit; Julie Mearkle for her strength; Sara Forrest for her compassion; Nancy Franke for bringing a new perspective; Jeff Lohrius for being a good friend; Emily Millen for her enthusiasm. A special thank you to Olivia Weber for showing up in tears on my doorstep second year at Naropa in need of help with a statistics paper and for trying to pay me back ever since with constant love and support through many changes in my life that would have felt insurmountable without an amazing friend by my side.

Kristina Bechtoldt for being there whenever I call no matter how long it's been since we last spoke. Kathleen Thompson for being a persistent friend even when I didn't know I needed one. Misa Lobato for living next to me, working out with me, and rescuing my plants one crazy summer. Beth Topf for calling, caring, and always being there. Erin Brindle for all the wonderful lunch dates.

DISCLAIMER

The case studies, stories, contributions, and vignettes in this book are true in spirit. Details have been changed and some stories are a mix of several accounts in order to protect the confidentiality of the people and facilities involved. Regardless, consent forms were obtained in every instance as an added measure to treat all material in an ethical and professional way.

When the Phoenix resurrects from the ashes, she is stronger and more extraordinary than ever before.

INTRODUCTION

I still remember when I was four sitting on a table playing with plastic bead necklaces or costume jewelry when Mama brought library books to an old lady in an apartment building when I was really little. I don't remember the woman we visited, but Mama said I asked about her for months after she died. Now I have this one vivid image, alive with feeling, which has traveled with me my entire life.

Emery

Welcome! This is the culmination of several years of writing about the vast and varied experiences that can come with self-employment and independent contracting. The way I work has changed several times throughout this process and the approaches have proven useful over and over again. If you take nothing else away with you, I hope you learn to jump in and try out something new. Rarely will everything go as we originally pictured it. I always thought I would write a book in my studio, surrounded by art supplies and inspiration. Little did I know that inspiration and writing would happen in coffee houses, libraries, 30,000 feet in the air, on my couch when art projects took over the table, visiting parents and friends, and finally during train rides along the Hudson to upstate New York. Don't wait for the perfect time and way to do whatever it is you would love to do because you will miss out on the adventure and spontaneity of the journey!

Emery Hurst Mikel
emery.mikel@gmail.com
www.creativelyhealing.com

Mission statement

The main goal of this book is to mentor and, even more importantly, to inspire anyone wishing to strike out on his or her own to bring the creative and expressive arts to clients. This business structure and selection of anecdotes have come from what I learned through trial and error. A guide or even a rough outline would have been helpful when beginning my own journey into self-employment as an art therapist, so I hope this book helps to fill that void for you as you follow your own path.

A note about legal and ethical considerations

It is important for everyone considering self-employment to understand the ethical and legal issues that come with the decision to work for yourself. This book and all of its advice are focused on independent contracting. While many of the ideas can be carried over to private practice, there are some important differences between the two ways of working. In this guide an independent contractor is a creative arts therapist who contracts with a facility or agency to run groups or offer individual sessions within the scope of her training and experience. The contract, whether written or verbal, is made with the facility and the therapist is overseen and paid by the company.

I want to make the distinction clear because it is okay and good to be creative about how you work as long as you know where the existing boundaries are. For instance, the American Art Therapy Association's *Ethical Principles for Art Therapists* explains clearly that an independent practitioner is a credentialed professional member who practices independently and is paid by insurance or directly by clients. To be an independent practitioner the therapist must have and maintain her registration (ATR) and have worked clinically for a specified amount of time. For more information see Section 12 of *Ethical Principles for Art Therapists* at www.arttherapy.org/aata-ethics.html.

When I started contracting I was very careful to evaluate each situation and company to make sure I was following ethical guidelines and staying within my current scope of knowledge. I had a supervisor at each job that was my main contact and boss. I also had an ATR supervisor outside of work who I saw on a regular basis. If opportunities arose that conflicted with the principles I needed to follow I graciously turned them down or referred them to other art therapists and discussed the situations with my supervisors.

It is the responsibility of each individual to do the research and learn the laws, guidelines, and specifications for her profession according to the area in which she resides or works and according to the organizations, state offices or other governing bodies she is expected to answer to.

How to use this book

This book can be used as a step-by-step guide, a reference for questions, or just a good read as you venture into working for yourself. It is divided into chapters that generally follow the progression of preparing for, starting, running, and closing or transitioning a contract business. There are many books out there that focus on creating a business plan, budget, resume, and much more, so I have touched on these subjects and given some creative advice more pertinent for this audience, while also suggesting you find the resources for any areas in which you feel you need more detailed direction. There are some recommendations for books in the reading list, and remember to reach out to colleagues and friends with questions, or please feel free to get in touch with me at any point. Please also refer to the section "Adapting for various types of therapy or populations" later in this chapter.

General layout for each chapter

- Title page—A drawing and a story from my life that applies to the chapter coming up.

- Chapter—Throughout the chapter there are anecdotes to further illustrate the information and offer some entertaining stories.

- Brass tacks—In Chapters 1 through 5, following the bulk of the information, there is a section that covers the practical aspects to think about that fit within the chapter's theme. This will include topics such as liability insurance, dress codes, tax tips, and more.

- Creative break—Finally, at the end of Chapters 1 through 5 there are creative exercises designed to give you a break and offer another way to think about or connect with each part of your journey. Enjoy this section and have fun!

Use your creativity to build the career you want, doing the work you love to do. This is a guide to help you on your journey and smooth out a few bumps along the way. Nothing can replace real-life experience, so once you mull over the idea and do a little prep work, jump in and see what happens.

There will be bumps, so embrace them, learn from them, and then share them to help others along on their own journey!

Bumps happen when you least expect them, so, once you are over the surprise, refocus and see what you can do about it. Even in the final stages of this book, I was surprised by some of the issues I ran into with consent forms. There were a few stories that I ended up removing or adjusting because of the feedback I received. At first I was put off by others not understanding what I was trying to do and I took it personally. As soon as I stepped back and re-read the correspondence, I began separating myself from the personal investment I had in the stories and was able to see what others were taking issue with or not understanding. Eventually, in every instance, it made complete sense to me. I just had to drop my personal agenda and I could change what I was doing. I am very thankful that they were willing to speak up and have a conversation about it in a way that gave me time to understand their point of view and learn from it.

Some important things to keep in mind:

- If it doesn't fit for you or your situation, that's okay! Find out what does work for you and implement it. This book is a guide, not a set of rules.

- As you go through the book, ask questions. Find people who will have a conversation with you about your ideas. I couldn't have done this alone.

- If you disagree or think there's more to discuss, email me! I welcome all feedback and would love to hear your stories. This is just one way to proceed.

- Jumping too far ahead in the book might overwhelm you or create mental blocks that don't need to be there. The progression works because, as you move from one stage to another, you learn and will be prepared for what comes next. Look ahead as long as it feels energizing and inspirational.

- Write things down. As you progress through this journey, or even if you're just daydreaming about the possibilities, have a notebook or a place to collect the scraps of paper you write on. Get those ideas, thoughts, struggles, triumphs, and creativity out of your head and onto the paper. Even if you don't use them right now, you never know what the future holds.

Adapting for various types of therapy or populations

This book is written from my point of view working as an art therapist with adults with developmental disabilities, the elderly, and people who have Alzheimer's disease. However, the information can be expanded to include other professions and populations. It just takes recognizing the need and adjusting the structure to fit your situation. If there is a specific question you have or population you would like to work with and need ideas, please contact me and I will be happy to tailor my thoughts to your circumstances.

Creative and expressive arts therapists

The best way to approach this kind of work is to use your strengths. Develop your program based on the interventions, populations, and ways you enjoy working. The exercises throughout this book are based in visual art because that is my background, but, aside from a few specific art interventions and projects, everything can be applied to your personal journey.

Where is your niche?

Facilities

- Community centers/spaces.
- Nursing homes.
- Schools.
- Religious centers or churches.
- Public health.
- Private practice offices.
- Non-profit organizations.
- Arts organizations.
- Parks and recreation programs.
- Teen centers.

- Day programs.
- Inpatient programs.
- Hospitals.
- Homes.

Locations

- A specific county, region, or subsection of your community.
- Might be close by or an under-served area further away from you.

Populations

- Seniors.
- Adults with developmental disabilities.
- School-age children.
- Foster care.
- Adoption.
- Teens.
- People with dementia and Alzheimer's disease.
- Hospices.
- Cancer survivors.
- People diagnosed with a mental illness.
- Bereavement.
- Families.
- Couples.

What ways can you work?

- Groups.
- Individuals.
- Support groups.

- Workshops.
- Address a specific issue or open up to the more general public.

You can work anywhere and do anything if you put your mind to it and figure out how.

Expanding into a new population

When expanding into a new area of work or a new population, it is highly important to examine your abilities and decide ethically if this is within your realm of knowledge. Most likely, the answer will be yes! Sometimes, however, you may realize that taking a class or some specialized training will better prepare you for the area you would like to expand into. Talking with friends and colleagues familiar with the population or type of work can also help in the decision. It's not a bad thing to realize you need more training or exposure before doing something. It will better serve you and your clients in the end to be realistic about your areas of expertise. Also, it is always great to connect with new people and learn some new skills. You never know where it will lead!

Researching and adapting language

Research facilities, look at websites, and find key words to translate what you are offering into the language of the new population. For instance, when I approach groups that serve people with developmental disabilities, I change any section that refers to age and specifically Alzheimer's, but keep the ideas about serving the individual and focusing on strengths. I go to the facility's website or similar associations' websites and look for key words that are used to describe the population or main goals of the group or facility. Don't hesitate to ask questions of friends or colleagues to gather information.

Brass tacks

At this point in your journey, here are the key things you need to do.

Find your niche

What do you enjoy doing? Who do you love working with? What makes you excited to head out the door to a job? Answer these questions and then look into what is currently available in your community that addresses similar ideas. There are often small organizations or other individuals who will be happy to talk to you about your interests, and you never know when a conversation might lead to a new connection or a job offer. Find a place (I love coffee houses!) and try to have tea or lunch with a few people. Get to know what services are out there already and what needs still could use help being met. Where might you fit your services in?

Review ethical guidelines and your areas of expertise

Review the ethical guidelines for the work you do. It's important to remind yourself of where the boundaries are because you may come closer to them than you have in your previous work, or there might be new boundaries that are challenged in ways you have not experienced before. This also goes for your areas of expertise. It is all right to begin working with a new population, but at the same time it is important to make sure you are aware of the new challenges and issues that might arise. Find others to talk to and make sure you are prepared for the direction you are heading. If it makes sense or would be helpful, you should take a class or training in order to better prepare for your new ventures.

Remember that it never hurts as much to question something before you start down a path as it will if you disregard a little warning bell in your mind that later becomes a very uncomfortable or dangerous situation. It is important to admit when a population or situation is outside your scope of knowledge. See it as a positive decision. It frees you up to head in a direction that is better suited for your growth and, if you can refer the job to someone else, it builds community and connections. (Professional websites and links to their codes of ethics are included in Appendix C.)

I recommend reading the following books about ethics:

Art Therapy

- Moon, B. (2006) *Ethical issues in art therapy*. Springfield, IL: Charles C. Thomas Publisher.
- Furman, L.R. (2013) *Ethics in art therapy: Challenging topics for a complex modality*. London: Jessica Kingsley Publishers.

Music Therapy

- Dileo, C. (2000) *Ethical thinking in music therapy*. Cherry Hill, NJ: Jeffrey Books.

Other

- Taylor, K. (1995) *Ethics of caring: Honoring the web of life in our professional healing relationships*. Santa Cruz, CA: Hanford Mead Publishers, Inc.

Creative break

Before you are inundated with new ideas and ways to approach your life, take a few moments to reflect on why you picked up this book. This is the beginning when ideas are fresh and will act as your homing beacon while you develop and explore new possibilities.

Find a journal, notebook, sketchbook, or create a place on your computer to write down your thoughts, ideas, and responses to the exercises throughout this book. Keep in mind that there will be art as well as writing suggestions.

Writing

- What is your dream job?
- Where do you see yourself a year from now?
- What are you hoping to get out of this book?
- List five words that best describe what you want out of your work life.

Art making

Mandalas

On a blank page, use a cup, can, or compass to draw a circle.

Choose your favorite medium. (I love oil pastels or colored pencils!)

In the center, draw an image that represents you. It can be abstract or realistic (animal, flower, object, shape, or totem).

Continue adding to the picture or surround it with colors, however you like.

After you have finished drawing and coloring, think of words to put around your paper. These can be supportive words, words that describe your strengths, your goals, your hopes or dreams—whatever fits for you. They can be scattered throughout the page or in a circle around your mandala. Maybe there are some inside the circle too.

After you have finished, lean your art piece up against a stack of books or a wall and just sit quietly with it for a moment. Take in the colors, words, and images you see. What are you thinking? What are you feeling? Do not try to change your experience while looking at your art. Just notice it, name it (calm, nervous, excited, overwhelmed, etc.), and then let each observation go and see what comes up next.

First, just sit with it and then, if you like, you can write down some of your reflections. You can have a conversation with your art. Ask it questions and see what you get in response. Remain open. If it feels appropriate to just sit with your art, that is all right too.

Anytime you want to, you should pull this piece of art out and sit with it. Let it ground you or remind you where you were when you started this adventure.

Remember, there is no wrong way to do this!

A FOUNDATION

When I was eight, I loved visiting Grandma in the house on Bradford Drive. I would sit in front of the living room couch and write stories about animals and adventures. My parents said not to worry about how to spell and to just write it down. Then I would create bookmarks and sell them along with my stories for a nickel. I worked hard to arrange them nicely on the side table in the dining room so everyone would see them as they walked by.

Emery

Let's get started! It is time to develop a basic understanding of what this book is about. This chapter will answer the question "What is contract art therapy?" and offer a base of knowledge from which to proceed into the coming chapters. This is a great chapter to come back to if you ever need to feel more grounded or want to get back to basics.

Basic outline of the process

The process of independent contracting does not tend to be linear or cyclical. It's more like a round in singing. One line is started, and once a certain point in that line is reached, another voice is added, starting at the beginning while overlapping the first line as it continues forward. The words are the same but offset to create an overlapping, harmonious sound. In independent contracting we search for the harmonious flow of our work, as shown in Figure 1.1 on the following page.

Prepare marketing materials
and do research
|
Send out information
|
Phonecall follow-up
|
First phone conversations
and set up interviews
|
Run interview group and
schedule first paid job
|
Start jobs and   ⟶   Revise marketing materials
| and do research
Maintain connections with |
facility contacts   Send out information
| |
Build up projects and   Phonecall follow-up
interventions |
| First phone conversations
Find the monthly routine   and set up interviews
| |
End jobs when appropriate   Run interview group and
                      schedule first paid job
                           |
             Start jobs and   ⟶   Revise marketing materials
                           | and do research
      Maintain connections with |
             facility contacts   Send out information
                           | |
         Build up projects and   Phonecall follow-up
              interventions |
                           | First phone conversations
         Find the monthly routine   and set up interviews
                           | |
      End jobs when appropriate   Run interview group and
                                        schedule first paid job
                                              |
                                            Start jobs and continue the
                                                 cycle
                                                   |
                                            Maintain connections with
                                                   facility contacts
                                                   |
                                            Build up projects and
                                                interventions
                                                   |
                                            Find the monthly routine
                                                   |
                                        End jobs when appropriate

FIGURE 1.1 Harmonious flow in the process of independent contracting

In my work

I travel to places to serve people who, for various reasons, would not be able to travel to me. As I work, I explain to activities directors, recreation specialists, and other staff members how art benefits their residents, clients, and patients. Art therapy is offered in a way that is affordable to facilities that do not have the budget to hire a full-time or even part-time specialist. A sliding scale translates into asking those who can afford to pay a little more to balance out those who cannot, so that more programs can benefit from having art therapy.

Within groups I aim to improve quality of life, open up the possibility for expression, hear people who often go unheard, and be open to whatever my participants need in that moment. I once had a staff member remark, "You have to love this job because you can't be doing it for the money!" I think I've found a way to love it and make it a sustainable process. I love the uniqueness of each group and each individual. I like seeing the progression that, for many of my clients, happens over months, not sessions. When a person dies, often of old age, I find peace through my own art making and art therapy sessions with the rest of the group as we process that loss.

In my contract art therapy world there is constant fluctuation and change, but out of that comes such amazing growth. It does not matter if the person across from me is 50 years old or 99 years old. This is the most interesting work I have ever done and I hope to continue it for a long time yet.

Contract work vs. private practice

Private practice is a general term that refers to anyone working for himself or herself (i.e. not as an employee). However, contract work is not always private practice in the way it's understood by the mental health professions. Some professions or states may have rules regarding how soon you can begin your own private practice. I believe there is value in these rules and that it is also important to understand why they exist. Often what the rules or laws indicate is that you need more experience following school or certification before you can see clients in your own office alone. For anyone just starting out, working as an independent contractor gives the therapist freedom to be self-employed while providing certain layers of protection for you and your clients. This way, the spirit of these rules or laws is upheld when contemplating how to begin a mental health private practice. Always check with your state and professional board to find out what the rules and regulations are in your area.

No matter your level of experience, I believe that independent contracting can exist as a stand-alone business, a supplement to current work, or a way to move into private practice. There is a lot of flexibility built into this business model, and your contracting can change with you as your career and needs evolve over time.

A more in-depth comparison

Here is my perspective on the differences between a more stereotypical mental health private practice and an independent contractor's business. When working with companies or individual facilities, the contractor submits a W-9 form and is paid by the company that operates the facility. Payment is not directly received from the individuals participating in creative arts therapy or from insurance companies. Also, services are offered at the facility instead of in the therapist's office or home.

Always check on liability issues if something were to go wrong or a client files a lawsuit. Is the facility liable or are you? This is another determining factor when figuring out where on the continuum of private practice you fall. No matter where that point is, always obtain your own liability insurance before you start any kind of work.

See Table 1.1 on the following page for some more comparisons.

Here are a few places to start the research:

Art Therapy

- American Art Therapy Association—www.arttherapy.org/aata-ethics.html.
- Art Therapy Credentials Board—www.atcb.org.
- Furman, L.R. (2013). *Ethics in art therapy: Challenging topics for a complex modality.* London: Jessica Kingsley Publishers.

- Moon, B. (2006). *Ethical issues in art therapy.* Springfield, IL: Charles C. Thomas Publisher.

Music Therapy

- Certification Board for Music Therapists—www.cbmt.org.
- Dileo, C. (2000). *Ethical thinking in music therapy.* Cherry Hill, NJ: Jeffrey Books.

Other

- American Dance Therapy Association—www.adta.org.
- National Association for Drama Therapy—www.nadt.org.
- Taylor, K. (1995). *Ethics of caring: Honoring the web of life in our professional healing relationships.* Santa Cruz, CA: Hanford Mead Publishers, Inc.
- New York state—www.op.nysed.gov/prof/mhp

From personal experience, if you want to work in New York state, please do some research as this is one of the states with very specific rules and regulations which you will have to follow to practice creative arts therapy legally within the state.

Before you practice or move to a new state, make sure you find your state regulatory or licensing board in order to get answers to questions about scope of practice and registration requirements.

Table 1.1 The differences between contract work and private practice

Contract work	Private practice in an office
• The therapist is paid by the company or the facility.	• The therapist is paid by the client, insurance, etc.
• Services occur at the facility (home visit depends on other criteria*).	• Services occur in the therapist's office (home visit depends on other criteria*).

• The facility is usually liable if anything should happen to a client or in the case of a lawsuit. (This does not diminish the therapist's responsibilities or need to adhere to ethical guidelines. Always protect yourself by having professional liability insurance in case of unforeseen circumstances.)	• The therapist is usually liable if anything should happen to the client or in the case of lawsuit.
• The therapist decides on interventions and how art is used within the session but may have input from or discussions with the facility contact.	• The therapist decides on interventions and how art is used within the session.
• Payment and taxes: the therapist gives the facility a W-9 form (equivalent of a W-2 in part- or full-time work as an employee) and gets a 1099-MISC at tax time. If the minimum annual threshold isn't reached, the facility will not send a 1099-MISC, but the therapist still needs to report income, and either uses the facility's payment system or submits an invoice every month.	• Payment and taxes: the therapist bills/invoices client, a third party, or insurance. Files taxes under self-employment.
• Record keeping is important because the therapist is responsible for reporting all income. For the odd job here and there, income still needs to be reported, but the facility may not be responsible for sending paperwork to the therapist.	• Record keeping is important because the therapist is responsible for reporting all income.
• The therapist receives paycheck from facilities. No money is withheld from paycheck. Files Form 1040/Self-Employment tax at tax time. Schedule C helps figure out how much is owed. Estimated taxes must be paid throughout the following year if the therapist owes any federal taxes.	• No paycheck or no money is withheld from paycheck. Files Form 1040/Self-Employment tax at tax time. Schedule C helps figure out how much is owed. Estimated taxes must be paid throughout the following year if the therapist owes any federal taxes.
• Fees are flexible and determined by the therapist.	• Fees are flexible and determined by the therapist.

* If you do not meet the ethical or legal requirements to do work in which the client pays you directly you should find an agency that specializes in sending people out on home visits. Either way, boundaries are of the utmost importance when you work in someone's home. Make sure you set good boundaries, have a supervisor you can freely talk to, have liability insurance, and research legal and ethical guidelines for your specific location and profession.

What is challenging about independent contracting?

- The potential for a lot of driving and travel time.
- Having to continuously advertise your services and search for jobs.
- Building security into your jobs can be difficult.
- If something goes wrong, it is your responsibility because you are your own boss and making all the decisions.
- The need for constant self-motivation.
- Lacking consistent co-workers (it is good to have interns if possible).
- Needing a place to work and store supplies (i.e. a home office).
- Keeping up with invoices and paperwork.
- Not getting paid for sick days or vacation.
- Figuring out your own health insurance and taxes.

What is appealing about independent contracting?

- As an independent contractor, you can work in multiple locations with flexible hours and a sliding scale.
- You decide how many places you work, whether it's part-time at a few places, contractual at many facilities, or complementing a full-time job.
- Losing a job can have less financial impact.
- The ability to reach many clients.
- Adaptation and adjustment as you learn and grow.
- Learning about the many ways facilities operate.
- The possibility to connect with many staff members—and it's easy to limit time with those that you have conflicts with.
- The freedom to do many different projects on a budget.
- The potential to spread word about creative arts therapy.
- Flexibility in your schedule for sick days and vacation.

- It can be a stepping stone towards private practice.

- Case management is already in place and is provided by the facility.

- The ability to move between different populations (i.e. you can try a new kind of group to see if you'd like to pursue working with that population).

- Flexibility to schedule more time for your own art making.

- The ability to slow down when you feel the need for a break or want to settle into what you've built so far.

- The ability to speed up when you are feeling ambitious or are bringing new ideas to fruition.

As you enter this world, you will find new challenges and rewards at every turn. It is part of what keeps the work interesting and exciting. As long as you give yourself breaks and pay attention to balancing your time and effort, it can be a very fulfilling journey!

Brass tacks

Online presence

Do you have a blog? Website? Twitter account? If so, use this in your marketing. Sometimes the first impression a prospective employer has of you is through your website. This is the age of information and technological advances, so use these to your advantage. Remember, it is not enough to just have a website, blog, or Twitter account. You have to promote them and tell people they exist in order to have them work for you.

While keeping technology in mind, remember to check in with those you are working with to find out what is the most useful way for them to communicate. Some of the people I work with are comfortable with email but overwhelmed by other technology. Some of the volunteers or seniors can text, but "online" is an alternate universe to them.

Use the technology you are comfortable with to expand your connections, while making sure you are not leaving out key contacts who communicate a different way. Try a few different approaches and you will find the balance that makes the most sense to you.

Taxes

I have used TurboTax for the past few years and I love it. It makes the process easy but also leads you through the details so you can see what you are doing. If you have an accountant or a small business lawyer, ask them for advice regarding your specific situation. As I move into more complicated situations, I plan to find someone well versed in the type of work I am doing. This is not only to make sure I am doing things correctly but also so that I receive the appropriate tax breaks. When you first start and have a fairly straightforward situation, you can do your taxes on your own, but at a certain point it is very helpful to have the advice of someone who really understands the work.

Helpful links
TurboTax

- www.turbotax.intuit.com.

IRS

- www.irs.gov.
- www.irs.gov/Businesses/Small-Businesses-&-Self-Employed.
- www.irs.gov/Forms-&-Pubs.

➡ Creative break

Materials:

- drawing or collage supplies
- a blank piece of paper and a piece of tracing paper or clear plastic of the same size
- permanent markers.

First, create a picture of yourself.

It can be a stick figure or a fully developed colorful drawing. If you have a photo, you can collage yourself into the art.

Next, add images or words.

What are your strengths? What gives you energy and power? How have people described you in the past? These words and images can be surrounding and comforting you, or they may be flying into the air so everyone can see. Add them to your art piece as it makes sense for you.

Finally, on your piece of tracing paper or clear plastic, write the worries and fears you face. Cover the entire piece of plastic.

You can write a paragraph or sentences. It can be words just jumbled up. Large print or small. If you get stuck, just go with stream of consciousness. What have people said to you in the past that has brought you down or made you doubt yourself? What have you told yourself?

PAUSE HERE! Read the following after you have created the artwork.

Put your self-portrait in front of you and pause a moment to take it in. Now, cover it with your fears. These are some of the things that may come up, hold you back, or get in the way. They are important in their own right and alert us to various things we need to pay attention to, but at some point we need to decide how to move on either by dealing with or by dismissing the worries and fears. Take the fears off your artwork and see yourself, the way you are, as you deal with the challenges that arise to reach your goals and let yourself shine through!

Refer back to this any time you need to feel more grounded or when you feel stuck. It might remind you how to move through the fears or uncertainties.

START-UP AND JOB HUNTING

My adventures in high school began when I was 14 years old. While attanding the Madeira School I learned a lot about myself and the world around me, including many lessons, some more concrete than others. There is one piece of advice in particular that I took to heart. Our School motto and our mascot continue to help me through the many challenges that arise in life.

Emery

"Festina lente"—Make haste slowly.

Congratulations!

You have taken the first step towards a fulfilling and flexible way of working. Remember, this can go as quickly or slowly as you wish. Don't be afraid to step back to collect your thoughts now and then, or push forward when you're feeling energized and ready to go. Rely on friends, community, and anyone you go to for support. At any stage in this process, you can email me and ask questions, or if you'd like more hands-on interactions and supervision, we can set something up to get you to where you want to be.

In this section we'll explore how to find jobs and get started. There are several areas we'll go over that are about protecting yourself. Don't let these overwhelm you. The idea is that if you are aware of the possible issues that might arise and can set the appropriate boundaries upfront, there will be less hassle, fewer issues, and guidelines in place for you when something does happen in the future. Enjoy the chapter!

Marketing yourself: Part I
Building bridges

This is a time to build relationships. It's a balance between flexibility and not backing down from the things that are important to you or your beliefs about the work you are doing. There's no way to know ahead of time what kind of environment you are entering into, and each place will have its own feel, relationships, rules, and internal structure. The people you are in contact with at the facility often just need to feel heard and understood when it comes to their clients and concerns. So aim to be as understanding as possible while still expressing your needs and wants.

Consider the following. Is it all right with you if someone does not want to start for a few months or would like to try a few sessions at a lower price? How can those few months be viewed as an investment for the near future? When compromising, be very clear with what the expectations are.

> Example: "For the first three sessions I'll charge the trial rate of [$] and then for the fourth session [date] I'll begin charging the agreed rate of [$]."

Try to put these decisions and compromises in writing when possible, so that they are clear and easy to refer to. If you agreed to certain arrangements over the phone or in a conversation, it's smart to follow up with an email to confirm what was discussed. Email is great because you will have a written record of all of the exchanges you have with the facility contact. This will help to address any confusion that may arise in the future. Even better, in the email, is to end the above example with a question: "Does that sound right to you?" This will provoke a response and you will be able to show the other person that response if lines get crossed down the road.

If, for some reason, a working relationship can't be established immediately, is it possible to keep the lines of communication open for future work? Observing that things are hectic or do not seem to be lining up and then saying you will call in a month or two to try again can leave an opening without adding pressure to your schedule. When the start date is postponed, it is helpful to follow up a week or two later with a thank you note for the time they did spend with you and to remind them politely that you look forward to speaking with them again soon.

Trust with a backup plan

It's not necessarily that people want to take advantage of you; it's that we are all human and we make mistakes. The clearer and more upfront without judgment we can be, the fewer the mistakes and miscommunications and the quicker resolutions can happen. We get to know the people we are working with and we expect that they will occasionally double-book us, forget about a session, lose our invoice, or show us any number of unexpected strange behaviors. We will occasionally do this too, so we need to cultivate a relationship of trust and understanding. When a mistake is made, focus on showing compassion and coming up with a mutually beneficial solution. Also read the "What can you do?" advice in the section on termination in Chapter 5.

The backup plan consists of:

- clarity and details around expectations
- writing things down and following up on conversations with an email
- contracts and signed documents
- constant and consistent communication about any changes
- taking responsibility.

Soon after moving to Long Island, I showed up one day at a Jewish community center I had been working with to find the parking lot only half full and everyone going into the building wearing black or dark colors. I had a feeling something was different about today, so I gathered my supplies and headed in the front door. As I entered, I felt very much out of place and asked if the adult day center was open today. The gentleman greeting people looked surprised and informed me it was a holy day, so nothing would be open until Monday. I thanked him and returned to my car, feeling bad that I had just crashed a holy day. There had been a time or two previously that I was unaware of a day off for religious reasons, but my supervisor, Debbie, had always been great about alerting me before the actual day occurred.

I called and left a message for Debbie explaining I hadn't realized there was no program and that I would like to look over the calendar and write down all the upcoming days off to avoid confusion in the future. I also said not to worry; there was no charge as it was my mistake. I put a large part of the blame on myself because of my ignorance of the religious culture within which I was working. I immediately went out and bought a book so I could educate myself on holidays and traditions and gain a general understanding of Judaism. My elementary knowledge of the Jewish faith and culture had been enough for all the groups I had worked with previous to Long Island, but clearly that knowledge was no longer sufficient.

The following Monday I received a message from Debbie apologizing for not saying anything before the holiday and offering to pay for the group regardless. She said she had the money in the budget and that she knew I did research for projects around the holidays even though it was a different religion to my own. She reiterated how much she enjoyed the sessions and that she would be happy to discuss any questions I might have about the beliefs of my clients, should any arise.

While I still turned down the payment, I began asking more questions and took her up on the offer to help me learn more about my clients.

Persistence

Persistence is the most important thing, especially with the initial push to find jobs. When sending out a letter or even an email, there is no way to know who receives it, if they forget about it, if it gets lost or sent to the wrong person, or if it ends up in the trash unopened.

Therefore:

- Send repeat letters and call multiple times.
- Keep notes on when you write or call and any new information such as:
  - Names and titles (activity director, life enrichment director, etc.).
  - Are you calling the front desk, direct line, or personal cell?
  - Your impressions based on the people you speak with.
  - Any scheduling possibilities or likely fee ranges.
  - What is your gut reaction to the person you speak with?
  - Were you helped, brushed off, met with confusion, spoken to honestly?

You can learn a lot from the person at the front desk or the assistant who answers the phone. Keep track of your impressions while you continue to try to reach the right person. It's okay to stop if you are turned off by what you are receiving from the other end of the line, or to take breaks and try again later. Use your best judgment and trust your gut reactions!

> *About a year after I started building up my business, I received a call from a woman who was very excited about having me come do a free session and start up a program with her residents. After we talked a little, I realized this was one of the sites from my original list of possible jobs. That meant I had sent approximately five letters to the same place. As I was thinking about how amazing it was that my letter had taken five tries to get to the right person, the woman said, "Thank you so much for continuing to send letters when you didn't hear from me. I have been collecting your business cards for months now and have a pile on my desk to remind me to call. Every time I got a letter, I thought, 'Okay I'll do it tomorrow.' I can't wait to finally meet you!" She then asked if I would like some of my business cards back. I told her that if she knew of other people who might benefit from art therapy, she could pass the extra cards along.*

Time to make a marketing packet!

The first impression a person has of you can mean the difference between getting a call or not. It is important to be informative, piquing their curiosity without being overwhelming. The goal at this point is to receive a call from someone interested in more information.

You should include:

- at least a resume (one page maximum) and a cover letter
- a business card, if you have one—something smaller they can hang on to or put on their desk as a reminder to call you.

Other possibilities:

- a flyer or pamphlet with images about what you do
- a sample project outline with images
- one or two articles on art therapy, art with your targeted population, or other related material

- a copy of a presentation outline you have given about the work you do.

The bottom line is include information to intrigue, not overwhelm, your potential employer. Limit yourself to five pages as an absolute maximum, including your resume and cover letter. If *you* are overwhelmed by the amount of information in your packet, so are your prospective employers.

More in-depth tips:

- Resume (see sample in Appendix A):
  - one page maximum
  - clean, not crowded
  - includes an applicable objective
  - includes pertinent information and relevant training.
- Cover letter:
  - upbeat, positive, exciting, informative!

What can you bring to the people you are offering art therapy? What's your approach and why is this what you love to do? Focus on the strengths and positive outcomes. Try to avoid using negative language, even when making a valid point. Look at the examples below and examine how each relays a similar message. The first focuses more on the negative in tone and language, while the second gets the message across in a more positive, upbeat manner.

Example 1: "People suffering from dementia experience loss, confusion, and anxiety. Often they turn inwards as their abilities deteriorate and lack the outlets needed for a better quality of life. Art therapy can help with these negative symptoms and declining quality of life."

Or

Example 2: "For people living with dementia, art therapy can lessen anxiety, give back a sense of control, create feelings of accomplishment, and offer new outlets for expression and communication. For many, symptoms are alleviated and quality of life rises considerably after just one or two sessions."

In the first or second sentence of your cover letter, offer a free session. If you are lucky, the person reading the letter will get through a few sentences before deciding if what you are offering interests them. Even when they have made a decision, they are more likely to just go ahead and call instead of reading the rest of the letter. Offering the free session is risk-free for them and will draw in anyone who is even a little bit interested. There is more on how to prepare for and run the free session in the next chapter!

When you mention money, I suggest you say that you work on a sliding scale, but don't provide actual numbers, especially when first starting out. You never know when someone will offer you more than you expect. Keeping this topic open in your cover letter will offer you more flexibility later on.

Business cards

Often, when you give someone a business card, they will return the favor. As soon as you get a chance, without taking away from the conversation or exchange, make a few notes on the business card they handed you. A detail or two that will jog your memory will go a long way. At a conference you may get many cards. Designs or names might be similar, and it can be hard to distinguish one person from another once you are home again.

When creating your own cards, the design should express who you are, but watch out for overdoing it. The most important message to send with a business card is "Here is my contact information. You want to connect with me." Clarity is the key. If there is a design you just have to use and it is bright and colorful with a lot of detail, then consider having the design on one side of the card and your information on the other. It does not matter how ingenious your design is if no one can see how to get in touch with you.

Try to include your name, job title and/or credentials, and at least an email address. Depending on who you expect to give these to, you can have a website, Twitter ID, or office address. There are so many inexpensive ways to purchase business cards, so I suggest starting with something basic and then, as you see what your requirements are, you can get new cards to suit your various situations or contact needs. Think about it before you add an address or phone number, and decide if it is okay for clients or others to have that information and to pass it along to people you do not know. When in doubt, leave them off and then write them on the card if the occasion calls for it. I like to have the back blank for just that reason. I can write notes to suit the needs of the person I am handing my card to. Some colleagues have an appointment reminder or calendar on the back and I can see how that could be useful as well.

Here are some helpful websites:

- www.us.moo.com (make sure you check out their MiniCards!).
- www.vistaprint.com.

Phone conversations

Okay, it's time to talk person to person! Depending on how you feel about promoting yourself, this can be an easier or more difficult part of the process. I suggest writing some things down before you have your first call so that you can refer to them as you're talking. When first communicating with a facility, it's important to be upbeat and positive, and to appear flexible and open. At the same time, stick to what you know and to your plan. Having a piece of paper listing your strengths, general goals for art therapy, why you do this, and any other details that may help answer questions can allow you to relax more because you don't have to worry about forgetting or omitting anything.

For example, be ready to explain why you do a specific activity at the free session:

> "It's affordable and gives me an idea of everyone's level of ability for adapting projects in the future. Since I use it on a regular basis, I will be able to focus more on the members of the group."

If they are seeking something else, assure them that you will be happy to discuss their needs further in person after the free painting/drumming/dancing session.

> *On the phone with a prospective facility, the activities director, Lori, asked about the free session. I explained how I would bring in everything for a painting group and how I would structure it. We chatted for a couple minutes and I told her about the other projects I offered and would bring examples of to the free session. Lori said she was interested, but they already*

had painting every week and she'd like to see a different project. Could I bring in the quilting and fabric because she knew they would love that and be very interested in what I could teach them. Thinking it would be best to please her and the residents, I said of course and that I would plan on doing a fabric workshop.

When I arrived at the facility, there were 20 people, instead of the 12 we'd discussed, and no staff to help out. I ran around doing the project for 45 minutes and was exhausted, but everyone was smiling and seemed to enjoy it. About ten minutes before I finished, Lori came in, introduced herself, and said everything looked great. I then watched as she got her coat and left the building. I asked a staff member where her office was and left a note telling her how the session went, people's reactions, and my phone number. Even after numerous calls and emails to follow up, I never heard from her again. The project ended up costing me much more in time, effort, and money than my originally planned painting session. I learned to stick to my plan and to explain why if anyone asked for something different. There are exceptions to the rule, but it's important to weigh the pros and cons as you decide when and how to bend your rules.

While speaking with your prospective employer, listen and ask questions. What have the participants done previously? What do they seem to enjoy? What would you say their level of functioning is? Are scissors or anything sharp allowed?

By asking concrete questions you can gauge the type of group you will need to run. Just remember that you want to get clear answers that relate to your specific objectives. General questions will be more likely to get generic answers. As you discuss the free session, ask about meeting with your potential supervisor right after the group to discuss how it went, what she thought, and future scheduling.

This is also your chance to find out about your clients' level of functioning. It can be a very subjective topic, but many people will present it as objective fact. Take note of what they say. Keep it in mind and then make your own evaluation. Ask questions that will give you helpful information. For example:

- What art materials have they used before?

- Is everyone capable of using scissors?

- How talkative is the group?

- Are they in wheelchairs and can they move around the room on their own?

Money

The topic of money will come up either during your phone conversation or at your first meeting. Have a range in mind and say you work on a sliding scale. If this is your first job, you can always say: "There's a wide range. Some of my colleagues make [$100] an hour and others more or less." Make sure the number you give in the [$] is something you are willing to accept. Or say: "I charge between [$50 and $150]. What can you do in that range?" Remember, while you do not want to undersell yourself, the question you are asking is: "How much is your *time* worth?" not "How much are *you* worth?"

You are priceless, so begin separating your personal worth from your work. Otherwise, you'll always feel underpaid or under-appreciated, and it will be that much more difficult when you inevitably lose jobs in the future. You should let your personality, great ideas, and excitement for your work energize you. Celebrate all the accomplishments you have and hurdles you clear. When clients make progress or have a good day, make sure to acknowledge that and take it to heart. Then, as setbacks, losses, and negative feedback occur, take a step back to gain some perspective. Be curious about what you can learn from the experience. Examine what your role was in it and what you could do differently next time. As soon as you have done this, it is time to let the negative feelings go and move on with your new-found knowledge.

When working for yourself, it's difficult to keep this perspective because you don't have co-workers and others around to help separate you from your work on a continuous basis. There are ways you will be able to expand your work and many amazing prospects that will bolster your energy reserve and excitement about what you do. Just take your time, take care of yourself, and you'll be amazed at how things add up in the end.

Negotiations

Think about being flexible, but make sure you value what you offer at a high enough price. If you leave yourself some flexibility, you can always renegotiate after a period of time. Try to do this part in person. It is a little more nerve-wracking for you, but it will also allow a back-and-forth between you and your potential boss. When in doubt, ask for time to think about what you discussed. You can always call and continue the conversation the next day.

Here are some examples of creative negotiation:

- Suggest that a lower fee is fine, but they will have to buy all the supplies on a list you provide and be sure to keep them in stock.

- Offer a slightly discounted fee for multiple groups at the same facility.

- If they can offer your group once a week, they pay less than those who can only offer it twice a month.

- If you work for a chain, offer a deal for multiple jobs within the company.

What is included in your fee?

- Supplies.
- Transportation/driving time/distance.
- Preparation/clean-up.
- Notes/paperwork/reporting/invoicing.
- Site-specific requirements.

When thinking about how much you charge, you will have to take into account all the time you spend outside of the actual session and think about how much you would realistically be able to work every week. With the elderly, there tend to be very specific windows of time when people are awake, not eating, and ready to do activities. Add to that the amount of time to drive between facilities and you could be down to a maximum of one group in the morning and two in the afternoon, unless you work out some special scheduling by doing back-to-back sessions at the same facility. Regardless, you will have to think about your energy level. Can you do three or four groups a day without being exhausted?

How do you talk about money?

- "There's a wide range. Some of my colleagues make [$100] for similar work."

- "I charge between [$50 and $150]. What can you do in that range?"

- "I work on a sliding scale. Can you afford [$100] an hour?"

Once you have your first job:

- "At one place I make [$60] an hour."

- "Several facilities pay [$75] an hour and one can afford [$120]."

- "One pays [$120], so I also accepted a site that could only afford [$40]."

Aim on the high side of reasonable and do not say a range or price you are not willing to take! The person across from you is most likely only going to negotiate down.

There are pros and cons to set prices as opposed to flexible prices. With set prices, you can hand the people you meet a spreadsheet that sets out your pricing and discounts for various arrangements. However, you are locked into what you hand them. With flexible pricing, you have to go in and negotiate a little more, but it's possible to go higher than you initially expect. It's a trade-off either way, but if you can make a spreadsheet with enough of a range built in, you might find a balance that offers the best of both worlds.

Supplies included

Some supplies will cost more than others. Decide on your budget and work towards having your first projects include a lot of reusable materials. For example, painting can be done multiple times with only paper needing replenishment between groups.

Then add in the more expensive projects now and then. Find the balance that works for your budget. (See Appendix B for project ideas.)

Contact list and notes

Keep track of the places you contact and the information you get. As you build your business, a spreadsheet of where you work, contact person, hourly rate, and other pertinent information can be useful. I always carry a copy in my planner or bag, so, I can quickly find the answer if I'm asked a question.

Site	$/hr.	Freq.	Contact	Phone #
The Regency	100	1/mo	George S.	(516) 346-5555
Sunrise	50	3/wk	Lynn	(631) 271-5555
Glen Cove	75	1/wk	Melanie J.	(703) 759-5555

Also keep a running list of places to send information, when you send it, to whom, and anything you hear back. This is a more complete sheet than the example above. Think of the contact list as a cheat sheet for places you are currently working and this business log as your complete record of what you are doing while running your business.

The Arbors at Jericho	Sent Packets: 9/15, 10/30, 11/16
Attn: Activities	Called: 11/15, 12/5
376 Jericho Street	Tried sending to Activities
Jericho, NY 11111	Director and Human Resources.
	During call on 11/15 was told to
(516) 333-5555	try Diane Smith the Recreation
D's direct line (516) 478-5555	Director. Resent packet to Diane
	on 11/16. Called 12/5. Free
	interview group set up for 1/15!

Contracts and agreements

Many places I have worked have not been open to a contract, which seems odd since they are hiring a "contractor." I think the people I have dealt with have baulked at signing a form committing them to something they are unfamiliar with. They want the flexibility to end my services if it is not working out the way they wished. In these cases, we hope they will realize after a few sessions how spectacular the services are; the idea of a contract can then be reintroduced. Regardless, it is important to protect yourself. Have a contract available and try it out at each place you go. Depending on the person you speak with, you can ask what would need to change in order to make it more acceptable or site-specific.

Since a contract is not always possible, I suggest at least having an agreement to be signed by you and the person you will be working for. You can think of this as a bill of rights that protects you and lays out the expectations of your relationship with the facility. Then you have a foundation of understanding to build on and a few terms worked out to protect yourself. You can also make the point that places that offer consistency and long-term scheduling and agree to contracts will have more flexibility and first choice when it comes to changes, events, and other options.

If you can pull together something that balances length and getting your points across succinctly, do it. If it is just not possible to agree on a contract, then be especially diligent in emailing, planning ahead, getting things in writing, and documentation to cover yourself in case an issue arises. (Samples are included in Appendix A.)

Brass tacks

Liability insurance

Going out on your own means protecting yourself. It's actually a good idea to have your own professional liability insurance when you are working for a larger company as well; as an independent contractor, however, it's a necessity. You may never have to use it, but it is there in case something happens and it will bring you peace of mind.

Research a couple of different companies, so you can make an informed decision. Pick individual coverage as an independent contractor unless you have actually formed a business. Generally, it should cost you less than $150 a year as a part-time contractor. As you build your business, you may need to switch to full-time status, and most insurance companies make this very easy to do. Here are two companies I recommend:

- HPSO—www.hpso.com.
- Allied Healthcare—http://ahc.lockton-ins.com/pl/covered Professions.html.

Health Insurance

Unless you work for a very progressive facility or can be a part of your spouses insurance plan you will have to look through your state's resources and be prepared to pay out of pocket for insurance options such as health, dental, and vision. The good news is that more and more companies are springing up to help out people who are self-employed and it is possible to claim some or all of the cost during tax time.

Look into unions and organizations you qualify to be a part of:

- Freelancers Union—www.freelancersunion.org. Has everything from medical to retirement planning. An applicant has to prove they freelance for a certain number of hours or make a certain amount through freelance work and the company is flexible about how this is shown.

Check to see what resources your state or local agencies have:

- California Employment Development Department (EDD) — www.edd.ca.gov/Disability/Self-Employed.htm. Has several programs self-employed individuals can opt into that include disability insurance and paid family leave. Some of the benefits to becoming a part of these programs involve short-term benefits when you suffer a loss of wages due to caring for a seriously ill relative or for non-work related illness, injury, or due to pregnancy and childbirth.

Dress code

It's important to dress professionally but also to consider that we are therapists who work with art materials or in unusual situations. Here is the philosophy I follow when traveling to facilities.

Whenever I go to work, I assume I'll be meeting the executive director of the facility for the first time.

I think about machine-washable but nice outfits for sessions (maybe a fun art apron on top!) and save the clothing I don't want near art materials for meetings, conferences, or presentations. The type of shoes I choose depends on how much walking I'll be doing and if there will be wheelchairs to roll over my toes. Other than that, I just consider the population I'm working with. Trust your common sense while letting your personality come out!

Ask what is appropriate at each facility. Some may have casual Fridays or do not mind casual clothing all week. Even if the policy is relaxed, think about how you want to present yourself.

Transportation and taxes

Expenses

Save everything! Keep all your receipts, preferably in order by date. Ideally, you should keep a spreadsheet of expenses by type (art supplies, lunches/food, car maintenance, etc.) on a monthly basis. However it works best for you, keep everything. A lot can count as a business expense at tax time, including clothes you buy for work, a percentage of your car maintenance, and even your home office if you have a room you use exclusively for your business.

Mileage book

Keep on top of your business mileage. A mileage book will usually have a column where you write your business travel and personal travel every day. In the back there will be space for your car maintenance, gas, and other vehicular expenses. In addition to what you enter, keep receipts or print off statements for tolls and anything else related to your car or transportation needs. Any office supply store should sell mileage books. I get the simplest, smallest version to keep in my car and it works out great!

➧ Creative break

Writing

Today's topic is value and worth.

If someone had unlimited funds, how much would you be worth? Write down some things that make you worth all the money in the world. These are the qualities that make you great at the work you do and bring that extra spark to your job that no one can ever pay you enough for.

Really let go! This is a chance to be completely self-indulgent!

Art making

Take five artist trading cards (www.artist-trading-cards.ch) or paper approximately 2½ × 3½ inches. Or draw the rectangle in your sketchbook. If you want to cut them down to be square, that's okay too. Create the following images on the cards:

- Card 1—you as a creative arts therapist.
- Card 2—an open and caring environment.
- Card 3—a stifling and harsh environment.
- Card 4—clients that you love working with.
- Card 5—clients that challenge you the most.

You can also combine cards (2 and 3 or 4 and 5) by creating the images on both sides of the card, or write something on the back of each card. Let this be a way to explore these topics with art materials. Abstract or realistic, use line, shape, and color to express your reactions to the above statements. If you get stuck, find something to trace a small circle on your card and use the mini mandala as your jumping-off point.

When you have finished, look at each card, one at a time. Reflect on the lines, shapes, and colors. Pay attention to what emotions or reactions you have to each card. Now look through all of them together and observe what similarities and differences there are in the designs and your reactions as you compare them. This is a good exercise when trying to see things from a new perspective or to give yourself a new way to relate to challenges coming up. It's also a fun way to record how you are feeling and dealing with various situations. Art cards are a great way to explore ideas in a smaller format. I suggest doing this exercise again a few months from now to see how things have changed.

Have fun while working!

When you need a break as you work through all your business needs, focus on the fun side of what you're doing:

- Create a logo.

- Design your invoices.

- Make samples of the projects you'll be doing.

- Do research.

- Read articles, books, and blogs.

All of these are things you should be doing, so don't let the fact that they can be fun lessen their importance!

3

GETTING THE JOB

At the age of 17, I was busy auditioning and interviewing for schools, trying to figure out where I would be going to college. I remember the moment I was called up for my audition to get into Carnegie Mellon's directing program. They were taking us in pairs and had already called another person before me. It was then that I realized they had no idea I was a girl. My name doesn't point one way or another, and at Madeira, an all-girls high school, I had ended up playing only male roles in plays. As I stood up, the person holding my resume said, "You're Emery?!" I just said yes and smiled.

The other guy auditioning may remember this next part differently, but what I picture is the two of us walking down the hall together in Maggie Mo to the rehearsal room where we would perform our monologues. We were chatting, and, after establishing we were both doing the "dead in a box" monologue from Rosencrantz and Guildenstern Are Dead, he turned to me and said, "I'm doing mine with a British accent. What's special about yours?" I looked at him and said, "I'm a girl." Then we arrived at the room.

I was very happy in the fall to see that we had both been accepted into the program. He was an inspirational classmate and friend over the next four years and beyond, and I thank him for helping me stand out in a way I had never expected.

Emery

Okay, it's time to really jump in there and sell yourself as the brilliant, creative person you are! In this section we'll go over some things to think about and do when it comes to interviewing, running a free session, and setting yourself up to have the schedule and fee structure you want. Remember: be positive and energetic! If you can push yourself to really shine through this part of the process, you'll be able to relax more once you have the job. This is also a great time to call on that friend who gives great pep talks. Have a chat right before you go for an interview or when you are feeling uncertain about yourself. You can do it!

At this point in the process you have made contact with an actual person and are ready to get the job. For many types of work, this involves an interview to see if they like you and you like them. I have found that offering a free session as a part of the interview can really tip the scales in your favor as well as give you an opportunity to learn more specifically about the clients and their abilities. Offering a full hour will give a better picture of what it will be like when you're hired, but an abbreviated session offers a taste while saving on time and money.

Interviewing tips

Handshake

A good handshake can pull someone's attention to you faster than anything you could ever say. If the person you are meeting is distracted, a firm handshake will bring focus, and if the person is focused on you, a firm handshake leaves a great first impression. Practice your handshaking with a friend. I'm serious! I have been astounded at the horrible limp handshakes I get from the majority of the people I come into contact with on Long Island. A bad handshake gives a bad first impression. So practice and show the person you are solidly there and determined.

Eye contact

Look the person in the eye and keep direct eye contact as often as possible. Do not look at a person's lips unless you have to read lips to understand what is being said. Where you look and how you look say a lot about your confidence and attitude. If you look down every time you answer a question, you come across as unsure. If you look up and off into space, it seems as if you don't know the answer or are trying to make it up. You don't have to bore holes through the other person or make them uncomfortable, but, with practice, you will be able to hold eye contact and be relaxed all at the same time.

Sunglasses

Take them off! If you meet someone outside or if you happen to run into someone away from the facility, immediately remove your sunglasses. It's okay to angle yourself so you are not looking directly into the sun, but most important is to show you care and are paying attention by removing your sunglasses and allowing them to see your eyes and make eye contact. They will not even realize it matters, but it does.

Body and posture

Have you ever paid attention to how you hold your body? Do you tend to slouch? Are your shoulders back or up by your ears? Sit with a friend and experiment with how it looks to sit different ways. How do you feel if you cross both arms over your chest or slouch and look at the floor? Experiment and find a relaxed yet alert stance when standing and when sitting in a chair, so you know how you look and what message you are giving off during an interview. It may feel overly dramatic, but it will help you connect in a more meaningful way with the people who might hire you.

Attitude

Stay relaxed and positive. Laugh and smile when it makes sense. Leave any nerves or uncertainties at the door, and, when in doubt while interviewing, just ask a question to clarify the situation. For those who get extra nerves or a little freaked out right before an interview, find a way to diffuse your energy right before going into the building. I love listening to loud music on the way and giving my entire body a good shaking either in the parking lot or right before heading inside, depending on which is the least public space. Once in the building, focus and put everything else in your life on hold for an hour. Once you leave, you can freak out a little or expel more energy by running in circles. Set up a routine that includes whatever helps you stay relaxed and focused for the interview.

> I parked my car in the parking lot in front of the facility where I was about to run a free session. I had listened to my loud music and, of course, turned it down before entering the facility's driveway. I was feeling all right but still had some nerves. When I got out of the car, I focused on releasing my pent-up energy from head to toe, shaking my head, arms, legs, and entire body. It helped me feel a bit refreshed and ready to jump into the interview.
>
> I noticed a man walking from his car to the front door of the building and hoped he had not seen my bizarre expenditure of energy. He just smiled when he held the door for me, so I thought nothing of it. Five minutes later, it turned out he was the activity director and would be interviewing me.

I still have no idea if he saw me, but I jumped into the session and interview with a little extra verve just in case and had a new job an hour later!

Ask questions and listen

Have questions to ask and topics to comment on. Base these on the research you have done in preparation for the interview. Make sure you are listening to what is being said. Use your reflective listening skills and take what the interviewer says to form questions or comments. If he or she mentions how much work has gone into the art studio, then make sure to comment on it and point out something you are excited to see in the space. You need to relate both to the facility and to the person in front of you.

What to wear

Dress professionally. This is the first impression you give; even if using art materials, dress up a little more than normal. A favorite outfit that makes you feel more confident is great. Don't wear something you are not comfortable in. The worst thing you can do is undermine yourself, and an uncomfortable outfit can be a constant annoyance. Show them who you are in your favorite professional outfit. This means something different to everyone. My favorite outfit is a skirt that hides paint drips and looks great with my favorite brown boots; it can also be worn with any number of shirts. It adds a little boost and I feel confident as well as comfortable, in case they want to take me on a tour of the facility.

One morning an energetic woman, Diane, called and said she loved my packet and could we set up a time to talk. This was before I had thought of offering a free session. She was an art therapist and loved the articles I had included in my information as well as the types of projects I offered. I went in a few days later and we had a wonderful meeting. She asked if I could work several hours every Saturday and offered a great price, so I said yes. We agreed on a start date and I left thinking "Wow!"

I showed up two weeks later on the start date. Diane was out of town and no one knew anything about me. So I went home and called to say I would come by next week. No call back, but I went the following Saturday anyway. Diane was out for the day. A series of one-way phone calls followed with no response. I decided not to show up again until I had found out what was going on. I emailed, called, and faxed several times. After getting nothing in return, I took a deep breath and added the facility back to my list of places to contact. I sent mailings every time I did another round of marketing.

Six months later I heard from Rebecca, who had just replaced Diane and was interested in my groups. From there I began going once a month on the assisted living floor and once a month on the independent living floor. I mentioned there had been some miscommunication before and that I was happy this had worked out. It didn't feel right to elaborate and it turned out Rebecca and Diane knew each other and were good friends.

When things like that happen, I find it helpful to assume there must be something going on that I just don't know about, but it's also good to try to see the lessons on both sides of the story. I adjusted how I communicated with people following that experience by always being timely returning phone calls and never ignoring something, even if I wasn't sure how to handle it. If I needed to, I asked advice of others before responding, but I would not leave someone hanging. I didn't want to leave anyone feeling the way I had.

Marketing yourself: Part II

Interviewing is a chance to make a new contact and you never know when that will be helpful. It is important to be upbeat and flexible while holding firm to what you need.

Example

If asked, are you certain you want to be in charge of the bulletin boards? What if you're told you will be expected only to do projects about the holidays each month?

It's great if you are okay with those requests or limitations; then you can agree to them. However, if the answer is no, then explain why not or what you would offer instead and how you think that can benefit the participants and community. For example, maybe suggest an art bulletin board for those who would enjoy and could benefit from sharing some of their work.

Be flexible yet honest about what you are offering.

Preparing for an interview

Research the facility and know what kinds of programs go on there. If they have a website, you can find out a lot about the philosophy of the facility and what levels of care they provide. Be ready to share that knowledge when speaking with your potential boss. For example:

"I noticed on the website that there are several levels of care. If we can work out something where I do a group here in independent living and then one on the assisted living floor, I can offer you a price break."

Everything is a possibility, but only if you voice your ideas. Do they have support groups? Do they do anything for the families of the residents? Have they ever had an art show? When you take the time to do the research, you'll have more possibilities open to you and the ability to ask informed questions.

Also try to gauge how much they will be able to spend. If you're just starting out and have absolutely no idea, figure out a way to give yourself some flexibility, so that if you agree to a price and then realize you are underpaid, you can do something about it in the near future. You can explain that it takes a few sessions to get to know the people in the group, evaluate supply needs and cost, and to offer a fair price for everyone involved.

Example

"Let's do an introductory rate of $50 an hour. We'll renegotiate in [four weeks, four sessions, two months] after I know more about the clients' needs and level of interest."

On my very first job, I did a quilting project with the group. There were four people with me and we had a great time cutting out fabric, gluing, and creating an interesting quilt that they were very proud of. I had spent about two hours pre-cutting and pulling together everything I needed for this project. Not to mention the money spent to get multiple shades of many colors of solid-colored fabric and then some patterns to add variety. All for a free session.

Following the session I sat down with Sasha, the activities director, and we discussed the success of the project. She was thrilled and wanted me *to begin coming in once a week. When it came to price, I had no idea, so I asked how much she could offer. We ended up settling on $40 an hour. I was thrilled to have my first job! Then I began getting other jobs and found out that $40 an hour wasn't much. People at other facilities, even those within the same parent company as Sasha's, were offering a minimum of $50 an hour and up to $75. I hadn't really built in any flexibility to renegotiate; I also found that when I brought in projects other than drawing and painting, I spent most of the money I was making on the project.*

Luckily, I learned quickly and began bumping up my value as an art therapist. I also came up with deals for those who could have me at least once a week or could offer me back-to-back sessions in different areas of their facility. I learned how to explain my prices and what they included, such as materials and travel. All of this led to better balance between the value of what I was offering and what the facility could afford.

Free session project

What is the best project for you to bring in for a free session? It really comes down to comfort level and cost. Choose a project you are used to doing or materials you feel very comfortable with. Then decide how cost-effective it is. There's no need to add extra anxiety or debt to your life for an interview session.

Things to consider:

- Cost of doing the project.
- Preparation and clean-up time.
- How work-intensive is this for you during the session?
- Flexibility for different levels of functioning.
- Will you be able to get a good read of this group while doing the project?

Painting is my preference. This medium offers a variety of possibilities. It's not costly for me in terms of supplies or time spent on preparation, it shows me a lot about the people in the group, and I know I can think and observe during the group. It is just as important for me to interview the facility and participants during this hour as it is to make a good impression.

Pick a project you are comfortable with, so you can concentrate on anything that comes up during the group and not have all your focus and energy spent on getting the project to run smoothly. Also, using a project and medium you are comfortable with will help boost your confidence during the interview!

Example of an art therapy interview session
Structure

- 5–10 minutes—Set up and chat with the participants in order to find out more about them, gauge their functioning level, and give yourself a chance to settle into the space and rhythm of the group/facility.

- 30–40 minutes—The project: a chance to engage with and learn from the participants. General directions and praise, but also walking around to each individual and helping those who need extra guidance. Step back a couple times during this part and observe how it's going. If your potential boss is in the room, take a minute to engage with her once everyone has started. Ask if she has questions or wants to join in. After a couple of minutes excuse yourself to continue working with the participants by saying, "I look forward to talking more after the session" or "Excuse me, it looks as if I'm needed over there." Take the time to engage, but also show you are there for the participants. Towards the end of this section let them know when five minutes remains and you'll be holding up their artwork soon. Be ready in case of resistance and explain why you hold up art or the benefits of showing the art. "You don't have to show anyone else, but everyone worked so hard we can at least share with the others in our group."

- 5 minutes—Hold up each person's work after asking for permission. Tell (don't ask) each person to "tell us about your painting." If they don't want to, they won't and that's okay, but more will say a sentence or two if given the opportunity. Make a positive comment about each piece before setting it back down and then thank the person for joining the group today before moving on. It can be handy to have the names on the art by this point. I often ask a staff member to go around and write the names on the back or in the lower corner. Then, as I hold up the art and address the person, I can use his or her name. Just make sure you follow the format of the facility when it comes to using first names such as Bob and Linda or the more formal Mr. and Mrs. Smith.

- 10–15 minutes—Ask what they thought of the session and get feedback. Show examples of other art. This not only gets the participants interested, but it can also pique the interest of the person who might hire you. Ask them what they would like to do next time. Have them help, in whatever way they can, to clean up.

Everything that could go wrong very possibly might. Part of what you are showing the facility is how you deal with crisis and with their quirky clients—and still manage to finish in style! Be ready to adapt, adjust, and throw your original plan out the window if you have to. There's no need to have a contingency plan for every possible situation, but at least think through some scenarios, so you're ready to be flexible and have tools to rely on.

What would you do in these situations?

- You are shown into a room with no tables, no water, and 20 people who have early-stage Alzheimer's disease. Then the activity director is called away and there is one staff member reading a magazine.

- A participant is starting to get physical and acting out against you or other participants.

- No one in the group understands what you are asking them to do. They seem only to be able to understand one instruction at a time.

- A person doesn't want to participate, but the staff member sits them down at the table anyway.

- A staff member takes the pencil from a participant's hand and begins "showing her how to do it."

- You have a fabric project and are told participants aren't allowed to use sharp scissors.

- Everyone is falling asleep within five minutes.

Better yet, what can you do in advance to minimize what might happen? Here are a few ideas:

- During your phone conversation or email, ask for everything you'll need for your first session and try to get an idea of the people who will be attending. Set clear boundaries in terms of how many people you can accommodate and how many staff members you expect to help out. I suggest at least one, even with small groups. They know the facility and residents better than you do.

- Have ideas on how to adjust the complexity of the activity before you show up for the group. This will allow you to accommodate different levels of functioning.

- Don't assume the person you spoke with has the same definitions for levels of functioning that you do. What if her idea of "fairly high-functioning" is someone confined to a wheelchair, who only has the use of her non-dominant hand, but who can speak clearly? Ask directed questions—such as "Can participants use scissors?"—that allow you to assess what the group can do.

➡ Brass tacks

W-9

When you go to a facility for the first time, have a filled-out W-9 form with you, so as you schedule your first session you can hand them the form and get into their system sooner. This saves time when you submit your first invoice and avoids delay in getting your first paycheck (see www.irs.gov/Forms-&-Pubs).

Nametags

Use your logo and think about how best to represent yourself to the population you are working with. My first nametag had my logo, my name, and "Art Therapist" on it. Eventually, I added just my logo and my name in larger print to the other side, so the seniors I work with can easily read it. I would use the large-print side for work and the other for talks, conferences, or gatherings.

I also suggest wearing it around your neck. If the badge attaches by pin, you'll begin finding holes in your clothes. A clip on the back makes it hard to find a place to attach it where people can easily see it. Try out a few different possibilities and you'll find the way that works best for you, your clothing, and the people you see.

Fees and scheduling

This discussion may happen right after the free session, so be prepared with a price range and several possible times, just in case. While there is momentum and face-to-face time with your prospective employer, try to get something scheduled. Even if you only schedule a first session, it will help to keep things moving in the right direction.

Leave at least a half an hour between jobs, with extra consideration for how long it will take to drive from one facility to another. My rule of thumb is you shouldn't drive more than the amount of time you'll be at the place (one-hour session = less than 30 minutes one way). Of course, I have made exceptions for various reasons, but only occasionally has it been worth it.

➤ Creative break

Think of a few words that describe this part of your journey. Pick one that stands out in some way or choose one from the list below that you identify with:

- fear
- challenge
- success
- failure
- strength
- ability
- acceptance
- uncertainty

- adventure

- teaching.

Poetry

Now find a quotation or poem about that word.

On a piece of paper, either write the poem/quotation or print, cut, and paste it down.

Art

Illustrate and amplify the words that are on the page using images you cut out of magazines or by drawing and painting with other art supplies you enjoy.

Voice

Once you have a completed art piece that combines the poem and images, stand up and read it aloud. Proclaim to the space around you what you have been exploring!

Movement

Now move!

Close your eyes and move in place…move in circles around the room…dance wildly with abandon! Move in whatever way makes sense to you as you further explore the poetic art you have created. The movemnet might be small and close to the ground, still and swaying in place, large and dramatic, smooth or jerky. It is whatever you feel in this moment.

For those not used to movement, first move in a way you feel comfortable. Then try to push yourself just a little further. It won't take a lot to get your body engaged, so do what you can and fully commit to what you do.

When finished

At whatever point you choose to stop, stand still with your eyes closed and just breathe. Notice how you are feeling and what your body is doing. Listen to the space around you, feel your feet firmly on the ground, and just breathe. When ready, slowly open your eyes. Now look at your art and think of the word that started this process. Do you relate to it differently? Do you have a new relationship with it? What has changed? You can write these responses down or just become aware of them.

This exercise will dig deeper into topics and attributes you relate to. Pulling in multiple ways of relating to the word chosen at the beginning of this exercise can uncover connections to and assumptions about ourselves that we may not have noticed before. Use this project as a way to broaden your understanding of how you are handling this journey into self-employment. It can be a way to celebrate your confidence, courage, and strides forward, or a way to explore your fears and challenges.

Another option

Create two collages with poems.

The first can be focused on your strengths and dreams. The second can be focused on your fears and uncertainties.

After you have created them, follow the process above for each or have the two art pieces engage in a conversation. What would your strengths and dreams tell your fears and uncertainties? What questions would they ask each other? Both can learn from the other, so make sure it's a two-way conversation!

4

DOING THE WORK

From the time I was 18 until my mid-twenties, I worked most summers at a sleep away camp in the Pocono Mountains. I had been hired to live in a cabin and to teach archery and riflery. A week before the campers arrived, a guy sat down next to me and said, "Hey, I noticed on your resume that you juggle. We need another person to work on the trapeze. Are you interested?"

I had seen the highflying trapeze upon arriving at camp a week before. At the time the outdoor rig sat in a grassy clearing below the tennis courts and looked like a bunch of metal poles and cables with a very small wooden plank about 20 feet in the air. I had wanted to try it sometime that summer but thought it would be a fun one-time thing. I looked at the guy for a minute and said yes. It was one of the craziest and best decisions I have ever made. I learned by jumping right in, and that first time grabbing the bar and swinging into the air was terrifying and exhilarating all at once.

Over the next few summers I learned a lot and met some really amazing people. My favorite trick is still the knee hang, especially without lines when I can just swing back and forth upside down for a little while. One of the first summers, I was able to do a backend split and release to the net without lines. Exhilarating and freeing! The other side was teaching so many campers of all ages and watching them overcome fears and reach for new heights. It was one of the most rewarding jobs I have had.

Emery

You have a job!

This is what you have been working so hard for. Now it is time to get your hands dirty and really enjoy the sessions and people you are working with. While this is a thrilling time, also take a moment to breathe a sigh of relief. Even as you continue looking for other jobs or expanding, you now have a focus. It's time to try out some projects, get to know the abilities of your clients, and build a relationship with the facility. Finally, have a glass of wine with a good friend to celebrate!

In this chapter we'll go over project ideas, supply ordering, invoices, and other things to consider when you get a job. Remember that you will do a great job and that every group is different, so stay flexible and open to new experiences. When you run into problems or are unsure of how to proceed in a situation or with a client, find someone with whom you can work through it. A good friend or supervisor can help put things in perspective and ask you questions that will help you find the right path to follow.

Expect the unexpected

There's just no way to anticipate everything that can happen. This is part of what makes the work so interesting! Just stay in the moment with whatever comes up and do what you can. Here are two stories to help illustrate how interesting things can get.

A group with three lovely ladies in it had been working on a quilt for about two weeks and we were in the finishing stages. We were choosing and gluing the border and arranging the patches they had created. The facility was a locked building for those with Alzheimer's. I had a group that ranged from three to eight people once a week and I had been coming for about a year. These three ladies were my regulars, and although they didn't remember my name, they always brightened up when they saw me and followed me into the art room.

As we continued arranging things, Barbara was trying to move all the patches around and Shirley was getting annoyed because she had put hers where she wanted it. I asked Barbara to leave Shirley's alone but to continue with the others, and then reassured Shirley I would make sure hers ended up exactly where she had put it. Both women seemed fine, so I turned back to Rosa, who only spoke Spanish, and continued helping her cut the border. The next thing I see is Shirley get up from the table, walk behind Barbara towards the door, and, on her way out, smack Barbara square in the back of the head.

Barbara looked as shocked as I did. I made sure she was okay and then poked my head into the activity director's office next door to let her know what had happened. She was surprised too. We continued working on the quilt and Barbara had already forgotten what had happened. A minute later Shirley came walking in through the door. She smiled at me and asked what we were working on today. I invited her to sit down on the far side of the table from Barbara and, after the two of them exchanged smiles and pleasantries, we finished the quilt without another mishap.

Sometimes the clients won't be the ones who create an unexpected situation.

One of the Alzheimer's facilities I had been at for over a year was having a family night that included dinner and entertainment. Rita, the activity director, was organizing it and invited me to bring my husband and meet some of the families of the people I worked with. I was grateful she had thought of including me and looked forward to meeting the families.

The night of the event we had a wonderful dinner and were able to sit with two of the families I had wanted to meet. Meeting the children of my clients is always exciting for me and a great time to connect and understand my clients on a new level. After dinner we all had cake and then I helped arrange the chairs for the entertainment. It's important to know that up until this evening I had described Rita as eccentric and thought she had lots of interesting ideas.

As we sat down, a six-foot-tall by four-foot-wide block of ice was wheeled in from the patio just outside. A nice-looking man came in wearing waders and rubber overalls, and holding a chainsaw. He smiled and turned the chainsaw on. For the next 45 minutes he carved the ice with the chainsaw, sending ice chunks and snow everywhere, even covering some of the audience. The room was filled with the roar of the chainsaw and Rita running to and fro trying to keep the confused and scared Alzheimer's residents from getting too close while the sculptor worked. None of the family members in the audience seemed at all bothered. My husband and I just kept looking at each other in disbelief. At one point he even asked if we were in some alternate universe.

At the end of the sculpting, I was thinking how nice it was that no one got hurt. The residents were then invited up to touch the sculpture. Most were in their slippers and had to walk through puddles of water to get to the sculpture. Then, when they touched it, they looked startled or unhappy at how cold and wet it was. I really couldn't tell if this was an amazing thinking-out-of-the-box moment or just plain crazy. It took the carpet over a week to fully dry out and Rita said next time she would do it outside to protect the carpet.

Art therapy projects

Although it sounds appealing, you don't need every material ever made when you're just starting out. Pick 2–3 projects you feel comfortable with that don't require constant replenishment of supplies. This will take you through the free sessions and add variety for a couple of months to those facilities that hire you. Then, once you have the money to buy more supplies, you can add to your repertoire.

Great first projects (also see Appendix B)

Painting

Materials:

- paint
- brushes
- water containers
- low tack tape (blue is great)
- paper.

Once you buy the paint, brushes, and containers, they will last a long time. The tape can be used and reused before you have to replenish it. So the only thing you'll need to acquire on a regular basis is more paper (and water).

One way to save money is to buy one small and one large round brush per person in the group. Wait to add more diverse and interesting brushes until you have several jobs. Spend a little extra to buy good-quality (medium-priced) brushes, so the bristles don't all fall out and they will hold a point. In the end, as long as you clean and store them appropriately, they will last longer and save you money. Also, when buying supplies, look out for refills which are often cheaper. Sometimes this doesn't work out because you need some part of the original to make the refill work, but refill watercolor trays are cheaper than the exact same trays that come with a plastic case around them.

Pastels

Oil pastels work well on their own or combined with watercolors. I suggest a combination of thin and thick varieties. The thinner ones offer a narrower line and more accuracy, while the thick ones are great for anyone who has trouble holding objects and for filling in large areas.

Colored pencils

When you have clients who are detail-oriented, want more control, or who have previous art experience, colored pencils can go a long way to satisfying their needs. I suggest finding sets where the entire pencil is the color of the lead, so it's easier to tell which pencil is which color.

I use drawing and painting not only for my free sessions but also in between other projects. It's cost-effective and there are many things that can be done as far as interventions and assessments are concerned. With larger groups, it helps me save money and is faster to set up and clean up than more complex projects. Also, the range of a controllable to a loose medium is available within the realm of painting and drawing materials, allowing me to work with clients across a wide range of skills.

Building art skills

Even with my clients who have memory impairment, I have seen art skills develop over time. They may not remember that we did art last week, but their ability with a paintbrush improves and carries over from one project to the next. Below is one example of a progression I use between projects to allow art skills to develop even when changing materials and adding variety.

Drawing

This is a more controlled medium with the focus on fine motor skills. It only takes one step to get the color/mark on the paper. Start with a pencil and colored pencils, and progressively get looser by moving to pastels.

Watercolor pencils or watercolor crayons

Watercolor pencils or crayons tend to be a bit costly, so I only use these for individual sessions or very small groups. (Otherwise, I go directly from drawing to oil pastels with watercolors.) When you use these materials, participants can draw as they did in the step before and then they can take a new step by dipping them into water before drawing. Depending on the people in the group, this can be a good transitional project or it can send mixed messages about how to use materials. I have ended up with a handful of normal crayons in a water glass because the client remembered you put things in water before using them! The clients can also be introduced to a brush and water with these materials by drawing and then painting with water over the drawing to create interesting effects. This creates the rhythm of getting a brush wet before touching it to paper which continues to develop in the next step.

Oil pastels/watercolor

Utilize the drawing skills from before with the oil pastels to create a picture. Once everyone is used to the oil pastels, watercolors can be added as a second stage in the art project. Once a drawing is made with oil pastels, use the watercolors to paint over and fill in on top of the oil pastels. While learning the process of using a brush with paint and water, the chances of success remains high because the drawing creates boundaries and will show through no matter what happens with the painting. Since the oil repels the water, there are a lot of fun things you can do with this. Experiment on your own first so you have a feel for it.

Painting

Keep the skills learned from the previous stage of dipping into water, dipping into paint, and transferring to the paper. Now more of the focus is on control of the paint than in the previous project. Acrylics offer more control, while watercolors are easier for participants to rinse out and the paint is more contained in the trays. I usually continue with watercolors and focus on how to create a wash, then on controlled lines, eventually moving to acrylic paint once some of the basic concepts of painting are remembered. For participants in mid-stage Alzheimer's, my main goal is for them to get the paint on the brush and then on the paper. In this stage especially, I stress how abstract art is a great way to experiment and just as acceptable as representational imagery.

Tissue paper collage

From here you can shift into a collage type of project while utilizing the skills learned with a paintbrush. In this stage we're using watery glue (Elmer's or other all-purpose glue plus a little water) and a paintbrush to dip into the glue and put on the paper. If there are sight issues, a little food coloring or colorful paper can help to offset the white glue and white paper. Use the glue and then stick tissue paper to it. You can progress to also putting glue on top of the tissue paper to seal it down. My mantra for the participants is glue—paper—glue. We may first aim to cover a piece of paper with colors or use wax/clear paper as a base to create "stained glass." Drawing a shape for them to fill in—a pumpkin, perhaps—helps guide the process.

Paper collage

Start with pre-cut pieces of paper or magazine cutouts and use a Q-tip to transfer tacky glue from container to paper. This technique uses the same process as before with the glue, but now there is more manipulation of images and paper. Have pre-cut pieces such as tree trunks, leaves, and apples, so an entire picture or scene can be made. Continue to use glue in this way or progress to glue sticks or squeezing glue out of a bottle.

Collage can get more intricate and can move to participants cutting their own shapes when appropriate.

Fabric or mosaics

At this point the skills used can move either to fabric and the creation of a quilt or to mosaics and a more 3D collage. Both continue to use skills similar to the paper collage techniques.

Mosaics focus more on the manipulation of materials. Start with multicolored beans or corn kernels until you know who will try to put things in their mouths, and then you can progress to tiles, mirrors, sea glass, and other non-edible materials when appropriate.

Fabric brings in new challenges with scissors but otherwise is a lot of fun texturally and can bring up new inspirations and reminiscing. Using glue eliminates the challenge of sewing, and tacky glue works very well, so there is no need to spend the extra money on fabric glue. Using fabric markers for those who can't cut will keep them building skills while offering a higher chance of success.

For both projects, participants can make individual pieces or a group piece. Projects such as stepping stones can be functional and shared in the community. Quilt patches can be put together into a larger quilt to hang on a wall in the facility. Both ways are fun and can be very rewarding for participants. (See Appendix B.)

Transitioning back to drawing

If this seems like a good cycle, you can use fabric markers from the quilting project to transition back to drawing and start the progression all over again. It's amazing to see what has improved since the first time, even with those who have memory impairment. I have seen more enthusiasm and ability each time, even if there is no memory of having done it before. Some of this has to do with the rapport you have built and the trust the clients now have in you and themselves.

Build on the projects you've done to create continuity with the skills your clients are learning. The skills being learned through the art making are going to continue to develop and improve through repetition and consistency. Even when cognition is changing or Alzheimer's is present, the physical skills are retained in the body, and the sense memory will be there more often than not. They may not know who you are from week to week, but for many people you'll see their skills continue to develop and improve.

Supply ordering

This is not difficult after your initial time or two! Some useful websites are:

- Blick Art Supplies—www.dickblick.com.
- Nasco—www.enasco.com/artsandcrafts.
- Michael's Arts and Crafts—www.michaels.com.
- A.C. Moore—www.acmoore.com.
- Pearl—www.pearlpaint.com.
- Utrecht—www.utrechtart.com.

Brands

Crayola® may remind you of childhood, but they make higher-quality products than some of the alternatives. I tend to stay away from cheaper brands because I have had a very low success rate with the durability and quality of the supplies. Find your balance of quality and price, and don't be afraid to try a new brand now and then. For tacky glue, I almost always buy the store brand because it's cheaper and works just as well as the commercial brands.

Planning

Work out your projects and how many people you will have to provide for. This will give you a general idea of your supply needs. Look through how many sessions you want to do each project within a month and add in an extra session or two to account for the unknown or yet-to-be-scheduled free sessions. When ordering the supplies, I try to strike a balance between affordability and quality. Some dollar stores have great colored pencils, but I always buy my paintbrushes from an art supply store. It just depends on what you can find in your area that meets your needs.

When the facility is providing the materials, you have to be clear about your needs. Have a written request with prices and, when possible, comparison shopping examples. If it's an easygoing site, they may ask you to get what you need within the budget and they will reimburse you. Some places will hand you a catalog and ask you to write down what you need in order of importance.

During your interview make sure you negotiate the amount of supplies and budget for materials, and clearly explain what your expectations are. This cuts down on confusion and makes asking for supplies a lot easier in the future. If they say they have materials already, ask to see them, so you know if they have the quality materials that you will need.

Always be respectful, but firm:

- "You have a good number of materials we can use. I'll just need to order a few things."

- "Here is a list of materials I need and a chart comparing several stores prices. I am happy to order from more than one place to save money."

- "What is the easiest way for me to approach you when it's time to order more supplies?"

When you have a chart of price comparisons between suppliers and a clear expectation of who is responsible for supplies and how often supplies need to be ordered, it makes the entire process easier. Many managers will do better with everything laid out in front of them to support what you are saying. It is not usually that they don't trust you, but at this point in the process the more you can support what you're saying, the quicker you will gain their trust and understanding.

Location! Location! Location!

Bingo had been going on before my art therapy group. When I arrived, some of the chips hadn't been put away. I knew a gentleman in my group tended to put things in his mouth, so I just quickly moved them all to a table away from our work space.

Most sites will have rooms that are safe for their participants to be in, but it's good to have a look around to make sure your space for that hour is safe and ready for the people who will be in it.

- Tables and chairs—Do you have enough, do they wobble (raises chances of spills), and are they appropriate for the people coming to the group?

- Sink or access to water—Whether for washing hands or painting, a sink and water nearby are useful.

- Windows—The natural light and scenery, even if it's just another building, can be of benefit to your group.

- Lighting—What is available and is it sufficient? Finding out if anyone in your group has vision problems can help determine how much light is needed. Do you need to bring a desk lamp or something to enhance the existing light? Also, if you are working from a still life or setup of some kind, you may need to bring in a light that can be directed to create more dramatic shadows than occur with the general fluorescent lighting most facilities have.

The five senses—smell, sight, touch, sound, taste

- How does the space relate to all your senses?

- What can you do to enhance the space?
- Would music add to or detract from the session? Do you have access to a player and CDs or do you need to bring your own?

The sixth sense

- How does it feel when you walk into the space?
- How will your participants feel when they walk in?

Ask for what you need.

> I once went to a place where they showed me into a room in the basement, which in itself can be just fine. However, this placed smelled like mildew, was ten times too big for my group, had fluorescent lighting, and the chairs and tables wobbled. As the seniors entered, they would make a face and say, "I hate this room" and "What is that smell?" and some would just turn around and walk out again. After a few weeks, several members of the staff commented on how they didn't understand why my group wasn't bigger. I was pretty sure I knew why.
>
> Then, one fortunate day, I was bringing in a painting project. The sink was just down the hall, and as I walked into the room, I was shocked. This room was called "The Art Room." It had a sink, windows, and was a smaller, more intimate space. Walking in felt nice and friendly and there were no mildew smells.
>
> When I inquired about using the room, the assistant activities director looked surprised and said, "You'd rather be in there?" When I said yes, he immediately switched our location. I still don't know why the larger room, which received such negative reactions from the clients, was supposedly better or preferred.
>
> Just goes to show you should always ask for what you need. You just might get it!

Invoices

Create something that includes your logo. What facilities need included in your invoice might vary slightly. Some might have to have a signature at the bottom, while others may just want you to send it via email. The example in Appendix A shows everything I have needed to include at one point or another. Use what works for you. My philosophy is that if they want it via snail mail, I'll sign the bottom. If they want it via email, I just delete the signature line. For places I have an account number, I include it. After you do it once or twice per company, you will only have to adjust the invoice number, dates of work, and total cost each month. The layout I use means that the invoice can be folded and put in a standard window envelope. This cuts down on addressing envelopes.

Pick a day to send out invoices each month. Again, some places may want to receive your invoices more or less frequently, so adjust as you go. I started sending them out at the beginning of each month for that coming month. I have now switched to sending them out at the end of the month. The reason, especially in winter, is dates can be cancelled or changed. In order to avoid sending invoices out twice, it's easier to send them out after the work is done. Many places prefer the end of the month.

W-9

This is the independent contractor's equivalent of the W-2. It's very easy to fill out and I suggest doing so and sending it to the person you are working for as soon as you schedule your first paid working day. This needs to be processed before you can get paid, so getting it in prior to the first invoice is a plus. If someone says they don't need one, go ahead and send it with your first invoice anyway. The financial department will want it. If they say you need to fill out a W-2, just ask why and let them know you usually fill out a W-9. This is many people's first time dealing with an independent contractor in this way. Sometimes it takes meeting and explaining why a W-9 is the appropriate form. Depending on the situation, you may have to be insistent or flexible.

Darla, the activity director at a community center, asked for a free session. It went exceedingly well and we sat down to talk about future sessions. She said that while they would love to hire me, my price range was too high and they could only afford $35 an hour, although they hoped that in the future they could have me multiple times a week. I asked to think about it over the weekend.

I weighed the pros and cons. Since I had some space in my calendar, I called Monday to accept the price. I also asked if in a couple of months we could re-evaluate. Darla said no problem and that she would send me the paperwork.

What I received from her included an employee handbook and multiple forms to sign. I called her the next morning and told her all I needed to send was a W-9 since I was an independent contractor. I also said she should talk to the business office and that they should understand that process. When she returned my call, she said the situation just didn't feel right and she couldn't pay me under the table by using a W-9.

I had to decide how insistent I was going to be at this point. I didn't want the misunderstanding of how a W-9 works to continue for me or anyone else who came after me, and I felt I needed to work as an independent contractor, not as an employee, since that is how I present myself professionally.

I left a message for Darla explaining that I couldn't accept the job as an employee and that a W-9 was actually the opposite of being paid under the table. It is how an independent contractor makes sure her wages are reported to the IRS. My goal was to be clear and understanding while also standing firm. There was a worry that I would lose this job because I wasn't adjusting to their needs, but I felt I needed to do this even though I was uncertain about the outcome.

I received the call the next day saying they would be happy to hire me as an independent contractor. I have been working at the facility for over a year and it has gone from once a week to four times a week. It is one of my favorite programs and has some amazing people working in it.

Release forms and photographing art

Why have release forms?

At conferences and in articles, case studies and client art are used to illustrate the points the speakers or authors make. In supervision during school and after graduation, therapists share information about their work in order to learn, hear ideas, move past issues, and share accomplishments. For all of these situations and any others that include sharing client information, a release form is required. Once you have the forms, you still need to protect clients by changing names and other identifying characteristics when appropriate. Some of the reasons you may want to obtain release forms include, but are not limited to:

- educational purposes

- supervision, publications, or presentations

- discussing art therapy with family members or clients

- empowering clients by asking them to teach others through their art.

Just like when you work for an agency, you need release forms for everything, but now it's solely up to you to get them and your responsibility to adhere to the ethical or legal guidelines. This requires a few additional steps when dealing with assisted living facilities and people with dementia or any situation in which there is a separate power of attorney.

Suggested steps:

1. Decide why you need releases, what you need them for, and if it is in the best interest of the client.

2. Determine, with the help of the facility, who can sign their own and for whom you need to pursue a separate signature. This is not subjective, based on your and your boss's thoughts on who is of sound mind. This is a question of ethics and legality to protect your clients and, in the long run, you.

3. Ask the person who has power of attorney to sign your form. It might be the client, a family member, or a completely separate entity.

4. Speak with your clients and explain what the release form is for. Respect anyone who says no. It's okay to ask why and have a conversation about it, but make sure they know it's okay if they don't want to do it.

5. Write a nice letter to the family/person with power of attorney, saying who you are and what you do. Be positive and upbeat! (See the example in Appendix A.)

6. Include a self-addressed stamped envelope for easy return of the form and a business card for the family to keep.

7. If the facility will be addressing the letters, include a letter to the facility, a copy of what you are sending the families, and write your return address on the stamped envelope for each

client's packet, so that all the facility has to do is write in one address per envelope.

For clients who have memory issues of any kind, I always ask on several different occasions if I can use their artwork in presentations, supervision, and so on. Then I look at which way the majority of their answers leaned, along with comments or emotions they showed during each conversation. I really aim to put my client first and try to have an understanding with them before I ever send a form out to a family member to have it signed.

Furman (2013) has a very informative chapter in her book about the ethical considerations to be aware of when working with cognitively impaired clients. The case study illustrates the issues that may arise and how to work through them in a compassionate, straightforward manner. Very important for everyone who works with populations where this topic is a consideration.

When forms come back, I assign a case study name for each client and file them away. From that point on I use the case study name for the artwork I save, so even if someone else were to see the art, the client's confidentiality would remain intact. I keep separate computer files for each client and have found this leads to easy creation of presentations when it's time to make the PowerPoint.

When you photograph the art, make any notes right then and there, or reference where the notes are, so you don't have to go searching each time you use the photo.

(See the story at the end of Chapter 7 for more on release form craziness!)

Note taking and treatment planning

You need to keep appropriate records, especially now that you are on your own. For groups or individuals where your services are clearly related to mental health, you should follow either the facility's prescribed way to keep notes or the state/national ethical and legal guidelines. I tend towards DAP (Data, Assessment, Plan) or SOAP (Subjective, Objective, Assessment, Plan) notes, with treatment plans written out every few months depending on the group or individual. If a facility wants you to keep notes on site or make notes in their files, make sure you discuss compensation for your time spent doing this. Also, examine its impact on how you'll do notes on your own, release forms and photographing art, and future needs you might have for presentations. (See samples in Appendix A.)

Private practice

In private practice, when a person comes into your office, there are documents you need to give your clients within the first session or two. Follow state guidelines regarding confidentiality and informed consent. Usually, you can connect with someone who has been doing this for a while, or call the state mental health board to make sure you know the specifics of which types of forms are required. It's always better to ask for clarification than to assume you know and then have issues down the road.

Moon (2006) gives an expansive and down-to-earth look at ethics for art therapists. His book is a must read and for those going into contracting or private practice, Chapter 12 deals with some of the specifics you will need to know and incorporate into your practice as you get started.

Other situations

The challenge comes in situations where you are unsure about your role. This may be a job you take with an activities department in a retirement home where they say they don't need notes or the participants are constantly changing. These can be fun groups and I believe the people still get a lot out of even a single session, but it makes note taking and treatment planning trickier. I do treatment planning for the group in general and make notes more specifically on any recurring participants. I still use DAP notes and make sure to comment on who was in the group that day.

Keep notes and treatment plans even if a place says they don't need notes, the group is more of a class format, or you are called something other than an art therapist. Even if it's not required, it will help you plan and you'll be covered if something comes up that questions your ethics or legal obligations as an independent contracting art therapist. It can't hurt and can only help in the end.

A friend once said how nice it must be at the facilities that don't require paperwork on the art therapy groups. She thought it was a great opportunity to just be able to focus on the art making. When I told her I still kept my own notes and treatment plans, she was shocked. "Why give yourself more work when you don't need to?" I told her that I saw my art therapy business as more than each individual facility and, as such, I needed to keep paperwork on my clients that was both ethical and legal. If I had been on staff in any of those facilities, I would have had to do notes of some kind. Since I was self-employed, that job fell to me to do on my own.

Assessments

I like to do an art therapy assessment every month or two, especially for groups with people who have Alzheimer's or dementia. Depending on your affinity for assessments and where you're working, you may do a lot of them, none, or some frequency in between.

For Alzheimer's disease, assessments can often show the progression of the disease or ways in which the person is changing as the disease progresses. The PPAT—Person Picking an Apple from a Tree—has been very effective in my work with those who have Alzheimer's when used repetitively over time. Some other assessments that I have tried include the Bird's Nest Drawing, Diagnostic Drawing Series (DDS), Kinetic House-Tree-Person, and bridge drawings.

When using assessments, you need to make sure you are trained and follow the guidelines for the assessment exactly as they are laid out. With my population, I have used many of these assessments as a guide for directives, and when I do this I make sure not to pass them off as the assessment. As with everything, use your best judgment, make sure to do the research, and ask questions of those with more experience so you can perform assessments in the best interests of your population.

Marketing yourself: Part III

Communication

Stay in touch with the people who employ you! They are the ones taking a chance and supporting the work you do. Sending a monthly newsletter, handwritten thank you notes, and maybe something special during the holidays will create a more personal experience for everyone involved. While keeping up with communication it is important to consider the ethical issues and be clear about how information is relayed. Please read the section in Chapter 7 about confidentiality and ethical considerations in the digital age.

In a newsletter, you can:

- summarize the past month
- promote upcoming projects
- share some highlights from specific facilities or clients (but keep confidentiality in mind)
- use this as a way to make all your facilities into one community for yourself.

As long as you pay attention to confidentiality, you can send the same newsletter to all your facilities. Just make sure to say things like:

"Some of the more independent groups have been working on quilts and the designs are stunning!"

This keeps the language general but still lets everyone know what's happening. You can also promote things that are happening at one facility, so that others might catch on and ask for something similar. Or give general praise—places not doing what you're praising think that everyone else is and hear about how well it's working!

I have brought up topics from fee scales and policy changes to marketing in newsletters, and it has turned out to be a great way to get a point across without anyone feeling singled out. With that being said, there are some things you should do in person. Always double-check with yourself and make sure you are not just trying to get out of an uncomfortable conversation by hiding behind the newsletter!

In-service

This is a great way to spread the word about what you do! Once you have an informational talk or presentation written up, you can reuse it with just minor changes each time you give it. Offer this to facilities where you already work as a way to educate the staff and/or clients and families. You can also offer it in place of or in conjunction with a free session to teach people about the services you offer.

Annual picnic

Have one! It's a great way to interact with several communities at once.

Invite the people you work for, with, and/or families. Try some of these ideas:

- Have a potluck to save money.

- Set up art activities and a large group project.

- Give a talk about everything that's happened in the past year and what's in the coming year (specific projects or conferences at which you will be speaking).

- Give a brief in-service about art therapy, why you do this, what you hope the participants gain (both people and facilities).

- See if any of your sites will "sponsor" your event, either through money or space. Each art activity can have a sponsor and you should have the name of the sponsors highly visible.

- Have a raffle. See if someone can donate prizes, or stores can donate art materials.

Most of all, be creative!

➡ Brass tacks

Keep communicating!

You have the job! Now keep the communication flowing. It is important not to neglect your new boss. Usually, your boss is not your client. Your boss hired you and is happy you come but may not be in the group you run. If she looks at your invoice a couple months later and wonders what it is you have been doing, she may decide your paycheck would make a bigger impact somewhere else. Use your newsletters, emails, thank you notes, and anything else you can think of to keep her updated, so she feels involved and informed. It will pay off in the end!

The round

The two sides of finding jobs and losing them happen, regardless of who you are or what you do. In order to help this cycle have less of an impact on your livelihood, this is a point in the process where you want to send out another round of marketing packets. Only occasionally will you reach your limit and be working so hard you can't fit in anything else. Until that happens, keep the pattern of sending out marketing materials going and find new places, new ways to work, and new people to connect with.

Coffee

Do not underestimate the power of a connection. If you hear of someone in the community doing something you are interested in or who you think you might enjoy meeting, ask the person to meet for coffee. Half an hour or an hour is long enough to make the initial connection without either party feeling forced to remain if it's not working. If it is a good connection, you will have a great time and can plan to meet again. Friending someone on Facebook or connecting on LinkedIn is good but does not replace a face-to-face meeting.

This goes for your contacts at facilities as well. For the people you enjoy working with, make a point of mentioning that it would be nice to sit and chat sometime outside of the facility. If you have a great interview, but don't get a job out of it, you can still keep the connection. If you get the job and still like the person you work with a few weeks later, ask them for coffee and find out more about them. These chances to connect open up possibilities that are valuable even though we may not know why until further down the road.

➡ Creative break

This break is all about seeing things differently.
    Materials:

- glue
- scissors

- several pieces of white paper
- one piece of black paper.

Find a song you like or a piece of music you think is fun to listen to. An instrumental piece is especially good for this creative break. Listen to it all the way through. Now set the black piece of paper in front of you. You are going to turn the music into a visual art piece. Cut up the white paper and glue it onto the black to represent the music you are listening to.

For example, is this a flowing, winding, smooth piece, or is it staccato with shifts and changes throughout? You can use long strips of paper or short pieces. If it starts out loud and then fades, maybe your white paper starts out large and then fades away, forming a triangle.

Try to represent several lines of the song on your piece of the paper. I tend to move from left to right, but I have seen people go from the top to the bottom or spiral from the inside out and vice versa. Once you have played the song a few times and created a piece you are happy with, lean the art piece against something and listen to the music once more. Immerse yourself in the experience. Do you see the music differently? Do you see your art piece differently? What did this process bring out for you?

It is important to be open to different perspectives that come from those we work with or for. I suggest trying this project again in a couple of weeks with the same piece of music. Then set your two art pieces side by side. What remained the same and what changed? This type of project can be a fun way to explore how we see, hear, and perceive things. If you have a supervision group or friends who would be interested, decide on the same piece of music, then come back a week later and put all your pieces up. Listen to the music while you look at the pieces. I guarantee the similarities and the differences will surprise you.

A variation on this is to gather paper in a variety of colors and let your colors help frame the piece of music. Maybe blue is the bass line, green is the melody, and yellow is the higher soprano line that fades in and out—whatever makes most sense to you as you listen to the music.

5

ENDINGS

I began graduate school two weeks before my 26th birthday. While at Naropa University, I learned a lot about experiencing the present moment instead of just trying to get through it to find the next moment. The Buddhist-based training was woven into classes in many ways, including meditation, and this approach developed skills that brought an awareness to the work I was doing in a deep and meaningful way. It taught not only about the ideas behind the philosophies and traditions but also how to continually develop and re-engage with them in our own lives.

During internship my third year, I relied heavily on my training to help me grow and process the work I was doing with people who had Alzheimer's disease. The residents were almost always in the present moment and that moment was continually changing or shifting. The same practices I developed to help me work with my clients' memory issues I found applied to the times when someone was sick or dying. The ability to stay with my own emotions as I sat with someone else at the end stages of life was challenging to say the least. Meditation and breathing helped me remain present while sitting quietly, holding a person's hand or listening as a sentence took several minutes to unfold. It turned out that every difficult situation was surmountable. I have always been patient and understanding, but the uphill battle for me was in sustaining this type of work without burning out and remaining engaged for longer periods of time.

The courage to stick with it came from a wonderful woman, Ruth. We developed a rapport over the first month or so and had a ritual of sitting together after lunch every day when the rest of the unit was still napping. We would talk about her family, her late husband, the chronic pain she experienced, and her life as an artist. Ruth had a deep gravelly voice and it took her some time to form words as she spoke. She was usually bent over in her wheelchair but had no trouble using her legs to propel herself around the room and get to wherever she wanted to go. She had a feisty side and a great sense of humor.

One day we were sitting and chatting about her late husband. She was telling me how sad she was feeling and how much she missed him. She put her hand to her chest and made a fist in her shirt, saying, "It hurts so much…right here." I mentioned how great a man he must have been and how important to each other they were for her to love him so much. She said, "Yes, but now…it hurts so much more…I don't know if I can do it." I said I wondered if it was all worth it. Without hesitation, Ruth opened her eyes wide, sat up straighter than usual, took my hand, and smiled as she said, "Yes, yes it is… It's better to have loved and lost than never to have loved at all… The journey is what counts." It took her several minutes to get each sentence out and I was deeply touched that she would make such an effort to relay these feelings and words to me. She then pulled me close and, with tears in her eyes, said, "And now...we need hot chocolate." A huge smile spread across her face as she pulled me along and headed towards the dining-room table. I smiled back and went to get our ritual after-talk hot chocolates.

Emery

Marketing yourself: Part IV

Yes, even at this point in the relationship with your facilities and the people at those facilities, you are marketing yourself. How you end things can determine if you still have a contact and your chances of getting a job in the future. A job can end in one of two ways. The facility can terminate the relationship or you can.

A job I had for about six months needed to end. It was a mutual feeling because the staff was over-stimulating, which overwhelmed the residents, so no one would make art for more than five minutes, and the staff would continually draw for the clients, no matter what I said. As a result, interest in the group began to dwindle. On top of that, they only had a small budget and it was further than I wanted to be driving. For the last two months I spoke with my immediate boss, Darlene, and explained some of what was going on while trying to keep it upbeat. When everything was considered, we decided it just wasn't working right now.

A couple of months later I got a call from Darlene. She had moved to another facility within the same company that was closer to me, had a bigger budget, with residents who really wanted to make art. We set up a time for me to do a free session, and it went very well. Within a week I had a new job with a slight pay bump and a boss I already knew who was excited I was there!

Termination by facility

Best-case scenario

The best-case scenario is when your direct boss comes up to you one day and says because of budget cuts they can't afford to have you come in any more, but they would like you to take 2–4 weeks to finish up with the participants, so there isn't a sudden change. This allows you the opportunity to ask questions and speak person to person.

It shows a level of respect between the two of you and the facility's appreciation of your sessions and the value of your work. It also gives you the chance to look for a replacement job before this one ends.

Worst-case scenario

The worst-case scenario is when you get voicemail from the job scheduled for the following day saying, "We won't be needing you anymore"—and it's effective immediately. No explanation, no termination with clients, and a lack of respect. Then, when you call back to ask questions or discuss the situation, you never get a response.

What can you do?

Something between the best and worst usually happens. There isn't really a way to prepare for the abrupt end of a job, but you can put some filters in place to save yourself from burning bridges and to help get through the frustration, sadness, or anger quickly.

First, no matter what, give yourself at least 24 hours before responding. Respond during the day when you are awake, alert, and thinking clearly. Ask a supervisor or good friend to be a sounding board for how you're feeling and what you plan on saying prior to contacting your employer.

Second, when you are writing an email or making a phone call, think before acting and have a list of points you want to make. Even if it was a best-case scenario, it's good to thank the person for taking the time to talk with you and give you a chance to terminate with clients. Strengthen the relationship even through this process of leaving. You're more likely to be at the top of their list to bring back if it ends constructively and calmly. (Just a quick side note. When writing an email, don't put anything in the "To" or "CC" box until you are sure it is all set to send out. This cuts down on accidental sending!)

Finally, don't be afraid to show some emotion. Explaining your reaction of surprise or confusion can create a more personal response from them. Just make sure it's appropriate and not in excess.

Even when you have planned and thought through scenarios, something might pop up and surprise you. For instance, at some places there can be high rates of staff turnover. It is always a surprise when you walk in one day to find you are not on the calendar and a new person is in charge who knows nothing about you. This can be confusing and frustrating. Practice understanding and patience when these things happen, especially if you are suddenly faced with a potential new boss when you thought you were coming to do a routine session. Offer to do the session for free that day or schedule a time when the new director is available to see it. Turn your annoyance, confusion, or frustration into a productive interview. When you get home, you can always make art or go for a walk or to the gym to work out any leftover frustration.

If you suddenly have a new boss, resend your information so they can learn about you. Take the initiative because there is no guarantee the last person left your business card or resume around for someone else to see. The most important thing is to not panic! When unexpected circumstances arise, you can always hand someone your business card and ask if you can call them the next day after you have a chance to look over your schedule. Stay positive and open!

Remember, they don't know your whole story just like you don't know theirs. Try giving them the benefit of the doubt. Whether they deserve it in the end or not, you can make a private note about it on your contact list for future reference.

I received a voicemail from Dorothy one day stating that, starting in March, they would no longer be needing my services. She had called on February 24. It was brief, direct, and, to me, lacked any sign that we had developed a relationship. I had been going to this site for over a year and had been running two groups back to back on a weekly basis. I was annoyed and quickly wrote an email expressing exactly how I felt about all of this. Two important things to remember: (1) I have a rule that I must wait at least 24 hours to respond to anything that I have an emotional response to; and (2) when I write emails, especially angry ones, I do not put anything in the "To," "CC," or "BCC" areas. This cuts down on accidental sending.

The key things running through my mind were the sudden loss of the group for both the dementia unit and the lovely independent women who painted with me. Next was the realization of the sudden loss of steady income that this group had generated and the fact that there was no lead time for me to find a job to replace it before this one ended.

The following day I had supervision and talked it through. Having a sounding board that was both more objective and there to support me was immensely helpful. In the end, I called Dorothy back and, when she answered calmly, stated how surprising this was and my concerns for the participants. I also stood up for myself and said how this sudden ending would affect me financially; I understood that budget changes occur, but some lead time to find a job to replace this one would have been appreciated. Also, I mentioned that letting me know in person or in a conversation would have been more respectful than leaving a message. She was very apologetic and told me how she had hated making these calls and had only received the budget the day before. So I remained open and told her how I realized this must be a horrible part of her job and I knew she had no control over the budget.

We went on to agree that I would continue for two more weeks in a row and then switch to once a month. Three months later she called and asked if we could increase to twice a month because her budget had been partially restored and she appreciated my openness and willingness to talk about it.

Termination by art therapist

It's not always cut and dried. There are many reasons you may want to end something: budget cuts, unreliable boss, uninterested clients, too far away, or changes to your schedule. If you need to end a job, the most important thing you can do for yourself is to leave the door open. Even if something isn't working right now, there might be a time when that job could be really useful, so just keep the contact and a relationship of some kind.

A friend of mine, Cammie, had applied to work with a company that ran a contracting business connecting therapists with at-risk families. At the time she was unsure about her level of interest but thought it worth going through the process to find out if this was something she would enjoy. Although the company seemed great, she came to realize the commitment would be too much with her current workload. Brian, her contact, had said it could be several months before there was a family to pair her up with, so when she didn't hear anything, she thought everything had worked out for the best and put it in the back of her mind.

When Brian called several weeks later, saying they had some prospective work for her and asked if she was still interested, Cammie was caught off guard. She quickly apologized and said she could no longer do it because she was moving. When he asked where, she responded, "Budapest." Cammie was as surprised as Brian, but he wished her well. She still doesn't know why she felt the need to make up a reason she couldn't do it, let alone say she was moving to the other side of the world.

Have a backup line for when you feel cornered or need to step back and think. Keep it simple and end on a positive note. Always be appreciative and say thank you at some point:

- "Let me take a look at my schedule and I'll be in touch with you by the end of the week. Thank you for taking the time to call!"

- "Thank you for getting in touch with me. I have several special events coming up in the next month. Is it all right if I look things over and call you in the next day or two?"

Termination because of a move or career change

When you move or change careers, why not help out another person or two while ensuring your clients will continue to be cared for after you are gone?

When I was preparing to move to Huntington, NY, on Long Island, Lisa Garlock, Clinical Placement Coordinator and Assistant Professor at the George Washington University graduate art therapy program, asked if I wanted to post my business as a job opening. It had never occurred to me and I jumped at the opportunity.

I had a few responses from graduates of GW and was excited there would be enough work to create a jumping-off point for more than one art therapist. Since this was a new experience, I decided not to charge for this transfer of business. Instead, I came up with a way to transition the art therapy groups and meet over lunch or coffee to teach about the business side of contracting.

We went through a one-month progression that was an abbreviation of what I do with interns over a year. The first week was about observing and building rapport with clients, followed by assisting with the sessions. The penultimate week focused on co-leading all the groups, and the final week I assisted and then stepped back from the responsibilities.

I used the month to end with my clients, and projects were based on saying goodbye and offering each other small art tokens to keep when we parted. The facilities were highly supportive and very excited to have people who were willing to train with me. It was such a relief and I felt that I had done what I needed to for my clients before moving. The idea that there were multiple jobs where there had been none before also felt like a way I had given back to the art therapy and senior communities in and around the Washington, DC metro area.

Selling or transitioning your business to someone else can be a very simple task. It can range from a pure business transaction to a more involved training process. I think the next time I do it there will be a combination of training and selling, but it will depend on the person and circumstances. Consider seriously what you have built and the value it has. Selling your business is a great way to move on or expand. At first it was hard for me to put a price on what I had, and it seemed like overstepping to expect someone else to pay for my creation, but a good friend pointed out that it was my creation and I deserved compensation for it. In retrospect, I am glad I opted for training/ transition time as "compensation," and next time I will decide based on the circumstances what makes the most sense to me.

Overall, it was a great learning experience for me too. I needed to think ahead by a month or more in order to have everything in place. Not only did I need to give notice at my jobs, but I also had to make sure the people I worked for were all right with my training people to come in after me. When I asked, everyone was open to it and very excited that the art therapy programs would continue, but there were also questions about the new therapists that I needed to answer and assurances many places wanted about their abilities and business practices. Once I assured them I would pass all my knowledge along and be training in the business side of my work as well as how I communicated with each facility, it ran fairly smoothly.

When I had interns, I taught the general ideas behind what I was doing. Transitioning my business made it a lot more real because I was teaching what I did so others could then do it too. It was a lot of fun and also challenging in a new way, but, between the handing my groups off and looking over cover letters and such, I felt immensely grateful to have gone this route.

Self-care

Take care of yourself for any type of ending. Find something to do with yourself when a client dies or is discharged, when you lose a job, or when you end a job. The sooner you have these rituals in place, the better a transition you can make when one of these things happens. A ritual will allow you to process what is going on and deal with it in a way that helps keep residual emotions from building up. Even when ending a job for a good reason at a facility where you have left the door open for work down the road, it is important to acknowledge and process the shift in your life.

What do you do to self-care?

- Work out.
- Make art.
- Dance.
- See friends.
- Watch a soppy or action-packed movie.
- Light a candle.
- Write in a journal.
- Listen to loud music.
- Play soothing music and take a bubble bath.

Whatever ritual you choose, I suggest it have two parts.

- Part 1—acknowledge the loss (see story below).
- Part 2—let the loss go and move forward (see self-care examples above).

Since I work with seniors, the most common loss for me is the death of a client. I developed a ritual with my first intern around the loss of clients. During supervision, we would light a candle. Then, using fabric and fabric markers, we made a quilt square representing that person. We would also speak their name aloud and share memories. This was partly to remember them and partly because, as therapists, we don't often get to say their real names. After we finished creating the quilt square, we would say something about the person, decide when we both felt satisfied, and then blow out the candle. After a moment, we would continue supervision. This is how we acknowledged the loss and then continued forward.

➥ Brass tacks

Follow through

Make sure you follow through on a few things when your job status changes.

- Clients—Even if you are not given a lot of time, try to bring a sense of closure to your clients. This can be done in many ways, so find a way that best fits for you, your clients, and the amount of time you have.

- Artwork—Return art to its rightful owner. Make sure to take pictures if you have permission to do so prior to returning the work.

- Notes and treatment planning—Finish this up as soon as you can after a job ends. If it sits, you will forget about doing it or it won't be as fresh in your mind when you finally get to it. Just because you don't have the job anymore does not mean you can ignore this last step. Even when keeping your own notes for a facility that didn't require them, you should finish what you started. You can always make it a part of your closing ritual or a way to transition out of the job.

- Liability insurance—Double-check on whether or not you are working full-time. Since jobs come and go, it is important to keep track of what qualifies as part- or full-time for your liability insurance and to change your status with your insurance company when you cross over to full-time or back to part-time.

- Facility's responsibility—Keep track of your final paychecks. Make sure you only let a maximum of a month go by without receiving payment before you touch base with the facility. In most cases, there won't be a problem. Occasionally, something goes haywire, so the more diligent you are, the quicker you can begin to resolve the issue.

Marketing

As soon as you know a job is ending, get back out there and send marketing packets to some new places! Planning ahead or finding something to fill an empty time slot will help you to move forward while maintaining your workload. Make sure to update your resume and cover letter with anything you have learned or changed since the last mailing.

➥ Creative break

This is something I have used many times to help me with endings. We are literally going to contain the relationships and events that are ending.

Materials:

- a box, can, or container with a lid (I like containers the size of a cigar box or paint can!)

- collage materials (paper, mosaic tiles, magazines, stones, images, acorns, pinecones, shells, ribbons, fabric, etc.)

- tacky glue

- scissors.

Think about what you might put in the box. I put art cards and things that clients give me when I am leaving a facility and the things I make when I am processing the loss of a client. If you don't make art when you lose something, this box can be a creation in and of itself. No need to put things in it unless you want to. Start with the outside or inside. Sometimes it's nice to go back and forth between the two.

The outside

What do you want to see when you look at this box? Is there something inspirational written on the outside or images of things that comfort you? Maybe the outside is dark and mysterious? Use your collage materials and let the process take you wherever you want to go. It's okay to not know how it will look before starting.

The inside

This might be a dark place with very little in it or it could be lighter with fabric to cushion whatever is placed inside. Are there images glued to the sides? Any special shells, keys, or interesting ribbons sitting inside?

When you feel that you have finished, set your container in front of you. Clear a space so it is just you and your container. Now close your eyes and take a few deep breaths. When you open your eyes again, explore the box as if for the first time. What is the outside like? If you run your hand across the top, is it smooth or are there objects glued there? Then slowly work your way inside. If you peek inside, what do you see? If there are objects or writings inside, how does it feel to encounter them? If it's empty, do you think there should be something there or is the space all that's necessary? Take a few minutes to explore your container. At any time you can return to your container, add to it, or just take it in.

> One box I made was with Ruth when my internship was about to end. We decorated the outside together with paint and then wrote down all the sayings and wisdom that she had shared with me over the past year. When we were done, I put a picture of myself inside the lid and made a duplicate box for myself. On one of my last days I gave Ruth the box and we went through it together. It felt like a good way to say goodbye. It wasn't until six months later, after Ruth had died, that the box showed its true purpose. I heard from Ruth's family that she had died and they told me that they had gone to get Ruth's things. While they were there, the family and staff sat down and took turns passing the box around, reading the sayings and sharing Ruth's words of wisdom.

INTERNS

Following the start of my contracting business at age 29, I was lucky enough to have interns two years in a row from George Washington University's graduate art therapy program. It's said that we often get the clients we need, not necessarily the clients we think we want. I think the same is true for interns. I loved having both my interns and they both helped me grow as a professional in many ways.

My first intern, Genevieve, came at a time when I was still developing my business. I was only eight months into it when she joined me. She was intelligent, mature, interested in the transpersonal approach, knew of Naropa, and had similar interests to mine. She really pushed me to grow the business because she could do so much and was always curious and ready to jump into new ideas. There were some things I didn't have to teach her because she came to me with a solid base of understanding from which we could both expand.

The following year Kitty interviewed with me and I was immediately drawn in by her energetic happiness, youthful spirit, and excitement about this new path in her life. During the interview it was clear she was smart and well spoken, so I was eager to have her on board. I knew she came with less experience, but I had no doubt she would gain that throughout her year with me. I didn't realize how much I would grow during my time with her. Kitty really pushed me to look at the base of what I had built. Her questions were direct and to the point and had me re-examining what I was doing so I could more clearly explain it. It's important to look at the basics and where everything started from time to time, and Kitty pushed me to do that.

I learned a lot by teaching both Genevieve and Kitty about art therapy and the business side of independent contracting. I had to explain myself and answer questions about my process and choices that had just seemed right at the time I implemented them. It re-energized my connection to my work and helped inspire me to try different approaches or look at what I was doing in a new light.

Emery

If you are near a university or any kind of creative arts therapy program, find out about their internship needs. It's a great chance to pass on your knowledge and have an assistant collaborator for a year. Interns can enrich the lives of your clients while also reigniting your love for what you do. At times they will drive you crazy, mess something up, or stare at you blankly, but those are the best times for both of you to learn!

"To teach is to learn twice." Joseph Joubert (via Shifu Doug Moffat)

Supervision

Be authentic! Be honest. Don't be afraid to say "I don't know."

There is nothing wrong with saying, "I'm not sure why I do it that way. Initially, it just seemed like a good idea. Let me think about it for a couple days and we'll revisit it in supervision next week."

Below is a suggested timeline that lays out the internship for one year. It mainly focuses on a first-year or more novice student, but, depending on the intern, some areas may be accomplished faster or slower Adjust your expectations and goals as you get to know your intern. Each person will be different, so this is expected to be a fluid model that adapts to each person and situation. Just keep in mind that adapting and being flexible is one thing, while not meeting appropriately challenging goals could point to issues that need to be addressed. For more advanced students, you may want to use this as a first-semester guideline or checklist and work in the business aspects plus more advanced goals for the second semester. Make sure to have fun!

Timeline

September–November

These three months are the observing, assisting, and settling-in months. Over the course of this time the intern learns through experience what goes on in contract art therapy, what it's like to travel to sites, and how supervision will be run. For first-year students, it's important to remember that they are coming into this kind of work with possibly no background except the prerequisites for their program. Allowing time to acclimatize is important.

In groups

- Observing groups.
- Traveling with art therapist to jobs.
- Taking notes and asking questions after each group.
- Moving from observing to assisting and then assisting to co-leading some of the easier groups.
- Starting to know the clients and specifics of the population.

- What is it like to interact with people in different stages of Alzheimer's?

- How do you speak with someone?

- What are the intern's personal challenges?

- After a month or two shift focus from general understanding of how things work to more specific areas.

- Why do we do specific interventions and projects?

- How could we improve or modify these and other projects to better help our clients?

- How do we hold the attention of the group or what are some topics of conversation to keep everyone at the table while setting up?

- Are you presenting yourself authentically or are you inadvertently being condescending?

In supervision

- Ethics. This type of work is very different from other internship sites and it is important to discuss the ethical principles that the intern is expected to follow. Encourage questions and continued discussion throughout the year while most importantly leading by example.

- This is the time to set clear and firm boundaries. Having a solid foundation at the start will allow more flexibility later on, once you know the intern's capabilities and challenges.

- When traveling together, make sure to discuss how that time in the car should be used. Is it all discussion about the groups and art therapy, or do you have some discussion and then listen to music the rest of the way home? Whatever you do is fine. Listening to music is a good demonstration of how to unwind or self-care after a group. Knowing the expectations will make this a productive but still relaxing time together.

- Establish a style of communication that supports honesty and straightforward conversation.
    - Continually ask for more detail to help the intern go deeper into her understanding.

- ○ Encourage, and be ready for, questions that challenge the manner in which you do things. Look at your own reactions and figure out when it feels more personal because of all the work you put into this. Most often the intern is curious or confused, not trying to criticize your hard work.

- ○ Make art or use other expressive arts in supervision from the beginning. Have the intern use art as a way to process whatever comes up during her internship.

- Help the intern establish her own self-care regimen. Suggest exercise, art, and other things that have helped you work through difficult clients or tiring days.

Goals

Art therapy

- Introduces self and works with individual clients during the calmest times in a session.

- Assists art therapist with set-up and clean-up.

- Is able to help individual clients begin the project once the session has started.

- Can explain the use of art therapy to clients and staff.

- Handles being in the same space as anxious, confused, or frustrated clients.

- Can administer an art therapy assessment.

- Actively participates in supervision by bringing up personal dilemmas, bringing in art, and showing curiosity.

- Follows the structure of the supervision hour.

- Can explain the variations in structure and expectations between different facilities.

- Has an understanding of the art therapist's role within each facility. Can explain what differs and why.

- Understands the role and expectations of the intern both during sessions at the facilities and when with art therapist outside of sessions.

- Knows importance of, and practices, expanding art skills. Brings art into supervision and shows inquisitiveness around new materials.

- Can explain the importance of cultural competency, time boundaries, and consistency, and give examples from internship.

Business

- Understands the impact the time at facilities has on how well the business does. Everything from appearance and presentation during sessions to clear, respectful communication with staff members.

- Has been shown a schedule and can see the rhythm of each month plus starts learning how to keep continuity even when there are fluctuations.

- Knows when invoices are sent.

December–May

These months are for refining skills, deepening understanding, and moving towards independence. You're helping prepare the student either for her second year or to go out into the world as an art therapist. Depending on the intern, you can offer more or less of a chance for independence. Set goals for the final month of the internship that you work towards.

In groups

- Moving from assistant to co-leader and then co-leader to leader in some groups.

- Occasionally, the art therapist can sit off to the side for increasingly long periods of time to observe and take notes on the accomplishments and challenges the intern is working on.

- Interactions with clients should become smoother and a flow within a session should be forming.

- This is when the intern develops her own style and flow within a group. It may not match yours, so try to decide when to suggest an adjustment and when to let the intern develop in her own way.

- Challenge the intern to try new things or push some boundaries that may be holding her back. Don't let something slide because it's become a pattern or you think she picked it up from observing you.

- Be pickier about how the intern presents herself.

- Most importantly, balance the criticism with praise for everything she is doing well or working on. Constantly ask for feedback after a group and see if she understands what's happening before pointing it out to her. If she gets it, you can just support instead of criticize.

- As you near the end, have the intern create a way to terminate with each group or person.

  ○ For those with Alzheimer's or people she's connected more closely with, it may be valuable to have several sessions devoted to termination.

  ○ Making something the client can keep from the intern and possibly something the client can give to the intern can be meaningful to both people.

  ○ I have found that art cards are a great size for termination projects and decorating or making a box to keep them in can be a part of supervision.

In supervision

- The intern should be taking a more active role in supervision and bringing in art, both client and personal, to share with the art therapist.

- She should be demonstrating that she can use supervision to grow and learn.

- This is often a time to encourage independence and to challenge the intern to push herself to reach her full potential at this internship site.

- Set clear goals and work together to achieve them.

- Make sure to continually check in with yourself and your intern. This is a time when patterns have become set, and it's important to still be asking the direct questions about how everything is going. Don't let assumptions take away from the possible learning experience in these last few months.

- Begin teaching about the business side of everything. Depending on the intern this can start first semester, but I have found it to be a lot of new information for some.

- Ask the intern to start creating her own interventions and coming up with her own style of how to do things. If possible, try out new projects in supervision and troubleshoot with your intern.

- This is also the semester to work on any challenges or issues related to the intern or the specific population. For my work with the elderly and people who have Alzheimer's, I always have a supervision devoted to death and dying. We also talk a lot about self-care and ways to work with the death of a client.

- As you near the end of the internship, discuss how what has been learned can be translated to other populations or situations.

- Also, remember to spend some time on closure and termination within supervision. Creating art together or for each other can be meaningful. Ask the intern how she would like to terminate or what kind of art she would like to create.

Goals (December–February): Art therapy

- Sets up for easy or smaller groups.

- Begins sessions, gains group's attention, introduces and explains project.

- Can explain the use of art therapy to clients, staff, and families.

- Is able to facilitate three art therapy themes or techniques and can scaffold them to at least two different levels of functioning.

- Can identify and describe the main clinical diagnoses of the population. Can discuss and suggest how this may be reflected in the art and how art therapy can possibly work with each issue.

- Knows how to proceed when dealing with clinical emergencies.
- Is able to lead a group from beginning to end with art therapist observing.
- Has developed effective communication and listening skills.
- Knows proper way to conduct oneself during an assessment interview.
- Can define art as therapy, transference, countertransference, isomorphism.
- Can explain various approaches to art therapy and describe the art therapist's specific approaches within this internship.

Goals (December–February): Business

- Understands the importance of communication with each facility and employer. Sees how newsletters can help keep people informed.
- Reviews art therapist's resume and cover letter while learning about getting jobs. Creates own resume and cover letter with a focus on keeping everything clear, understandable, and upbeat.
- If possible, sits in on phone calls between art therapist and facilities.
- Can explain the importance of first impressions over the phone and when interviewing.
- Begins learning about free sessions and how to go about creating one.

Goals (March–May): Art therapy

- Can do treatment planning on own.
- Explores theoretical and personal issues in depth.
- Can identify own unresolved issues and the effect they may have on the therapeutic relationship.
- Understands own artistic strengths and weaknesses.
- Plans, runs, and completes notes for a group.
- Intern's professional identity becomes more solid.

- Can discuss own theoretical framework beyond art therapist's approach.
- Demonstrates ability to present a case study in a professional manner.
- Takes ownership of and shows an interest in continuing own professional and psychological growth.
- Can identify times when art therapy is and is not the choice treatment for various populations and situations.
- Understands parallel processing.
- Demonstrates a more general knowledge of diagnostic categories and treatment implications.
- In-depth understanding of the termination process and its effect on patient and therapist; for seniors, includes death and dying, how to process it, and the benefits of creating a ritual.

Goals (March–May): Business

- Comprehends and can explain marketing techniques.
- Learns about sliding scales and negotiating prices.
- When appropriate, attends an interview or free session.
- Creates own marketing packet.
- Understands how to market herself at all stages, including when fired or ending a group.
- Goes through several scenarios or current struggles art therapist is having and helps devise ways of dealing with each issue.

Sample end-of-year goals

- The intern will run a group on her own for four consecutive sessions, with the art therapist observing the first and last session.
- The intern will be in charge of one full week of groups, including deciding on projects (at least one of which she developed on her own), gathering supplies, all aspects of the session from start to finish, and leading a discussion with the art therapist the following supervision about her reflections on

how the group went, what was successful/challenging, and what to work on for next time.

- The intern will work with an individual, either on the side while the art therapist runs the group or completely on her own, for eight sessions. During the sessions she will administer one art therapy assessment, keep notes (SOAP, DAP, or whatever is appropriate for the site), and use interventions that build on the previous sessions and knowledge of the client. She will also obtain a release form if one does not already exist, so she can bring art into supervision.

Assignments

Readings

Throughout the year I had several dates where interns had to bring in a few articles from the past year or two that applied to something we were learning about. They would give me a copy and the next week we would discuss it in supervision. This not only provided a topic of discussion but also encouraged the intern to do some research that was relevant. As the art therapist, it helped me see research and points of view I may not have normally found or thought of.

Writings

Aside from DAP notes and treatment planning, I would occasionally ask an intern to write about something. This was usually an area she was having difficulty in or a way to ask her to delve deeper into a topic. The subject could range from death and dying to communication skills with seniors who have Alzheimer's. I always stressed quality over quantity and never wanted it to be long or laborious, but I did expect thought to go into it.

Evaluations

There were a few times throughout the year when evaluations on the intern were due. The evaluation was basically a list of skills and achievements the intern needed to be ranked in. Each skill was followed by a choice of boxes to check that included "exceeds expectations," "meets expectations," "below expectations," and "N/A." I would ask the student to write out her evaluation and turn in her write up a week before we met to go over it.

This is what I asked for:

Pre-Evaluation Assignment

On December 2 you'll hand this in and the following Wednesday we'll fill out the evaluation together in supervision after discussing each part.

1. Define EE, ME, BE, and N/A as it pertains to us this year at this internship site. For example, what does it mean to exceed my expectations? Why might something not be applicable?

2. For each skill, write the following:
   1. Accomplished.
   2. Struggled with.
   3. What should you work on next?
   4. Where do you see yourself by the end of the year?

3. List up to three skills you might excel in by the end of the year. Why? How?

4. List skills you will need to consciously work on because they don't come as naturally to you as they might to others.

Don't generalize too much. Make sure answers relate to you in this internship this year with me as your supervisor. Don't go for the easy answer! Push yourself. You can do it!

Examples of "easy" answers:

Skill: Able to introduce self and begin session.

Introduced myself to the group and started the session.

Knowing what to say first.

Able to introduce myself and start a group.

Having an intern can be wonderful experience. Make sure to set boundaries early, make art, and keep them curious. Most important for you is to get support from the program the student comes from. If you and the school are on the same page, you know you have an ally and aren't doing this alone. When questions or issues arise, you'll have someone to call. You will also get to know people who work in the program and you never know what will come up in the future.

Intern's experiences
GENEVIEVE

My first year internship in the GW art therapy program (2008–2009) was with Emery Mikel. She was still in the process of building her business and I had the unique opportunity to be a part of that process. Emery shared with me her successes and failures along the way and integrated this area of learning into our supervisor/supervisee relationship, which resulted in an incredibly rich internship. I believe that much of what I learned and experienced during this year about how to self-promote and network directly influenced my experience of successfully finding work as an art therapist post-graduation.

During my internship with Emery, I definitely sensed that I was getting a different kind of experience from my fellow students. Compared to others, I spent a lot more time with my supervisor; driving from site to site, facilitating groups, processing, making art together. While I saw this as a benefit, I could see how this could be challenging for a less compatible supervisor/supervisee match. Compared to my fellow students, I got to experience many different types of settings, including nursing homes, retirement homes, and community centers, which I believe helped me to become more flexible and able to adapt to a changing environment. However, because we were working with such a specific population (elders and specifically those with dementia and Alzheimer's disease), I made it a priority to work with children and adolescents in a clinical setting for my second-year internship.

It was quite a shock going from contract art therapy in non-clinical settings to a psychiatric unit of a large hospital. I had to learn how to write progress notes in a very specific way and work within the structure of a large institution; however, this stark contrast in internship experiences helped prepare me for a wide range of professional settings post-graduation.

When I graduated, I moved to a different state and a much smaller city with no existing art therapy positions. While it was my second-year internship that qualified me to work in clinical settings, it was my time spent with Emery that put me one step ahead of my fellow students in terms of actually finding work. Emery had taught me how to put together a professional and attractive packet of information, including a cover letter, resume, and one or two brief articles on the uses and efficacy of art therapy. I sent these out to every program and organization that I thought could benefit from having an art therapist. Perhaps even more important than what I had learned about how to see opportunity where others might not was how to expect rejection and not lose hope.

Within a couple months I had a part-time art therapy position at an intensive outpatient program for people with eating disorders, a part-time volunteer position doing art therapy at a day program with adults with mental illness on an organic farm, and I had been awarded grant money to conduct four art therapy workshops at the local behavioral health hospital. It was when several of my fellow students contacted me for advice on how to find work that I realized just how fortunate I had been to intern with Emery doing contract art therapy. While those of you considering starting your own contract business might be tempted to hold off on taking an intern until your business is more established, I urge you not to wait. The knowledge and experience I gained from interning with Emery while her business was still growing and developing has proven to be invaluable.

Genevieve Camp, MA, ATR-BC, LCAT, RYT-200
Art Therapist and Yoga Teacher, UF&Shands Eating Disorder Recovery Center
Gainesville, FL
skillg@shands.ufl.edu

KITTY

As a first-year graduate student, I was not sure what to expect from having to balance a full course load and an internship. All I knew going into the art therapy program was that I needed to have an internship working with children for a year and adults for a year. I wasn't sure what kind of population I would enjoy or want to experience, so I tested the waters by interviewing at a few different placements. When I interviewed with Emery for an internship working with individuals who were experiencing varying levels of dementia, I knew it was a great fit. We got along well in the interview and were able to have an intelligent conversation right away. Once I received the offer for the internship, I had a small idea of what to expect, but really had no idea what I was getting into.

During the course of my internship I experienced some challenges and also learned a lot throughout the year. One of the biggest challenges I faced during the year was getting used to a slower pace of working. I was accustomed to a fast-paced environment, always being on my toes, and thinking quickly. In this type of internship it was important to learn how to take the time to slow down and think things through, keeping a slower pace because I didn't want to lose the clients' attention or understanding with fast talking or swift movements. I had to learn what the clients needed from me and how to accommodate those needs by slowing down or repeating myself without becoming frustrated. The way we worked with this population, there was a thin line between therapist and close acquaintance. I took what I learned in school about self-disclosure and asked myself: how will it affect the clients if I do or don't tell them my age, what city I live in, or if I have a boyfriend? I needed to learn for myself how to balance this and was able to by the end of the year.

This internship experience was very rewarding. As I got to know the clients and build a rapport with them and my supervisor, I came to really enjoy going to work each day, not knowing where the day may take me. As I brought issues and successes to the table during supervision, I felt more and more prepared for my next internship. I learned a lot about myself and what I was capable of throughout this experience and do not think I missed out on anything because of the atypical contract setting I was working in. I was able to see difficult clients, easy clients, challenging experiences, and everything else you could hope for in an internship preparing you for the real world. By my second year I felt confident that I could run groups on my own and relate to clients while keeping appropriate boundaries. I knew that, with a great supervisor, someone I could turn to with an issue or experience, I could learn from my mistakes and celebrate my successes.

This internship experience opened up a number of possibilities for life after school. It gave me the confidence and skills I needed to seek out a variety of jobs related to the arts and creative expression. Since I was able to work in a variety of settings, including assisted living centers, homes, and independent living apartments, my internship experience showed me that there are ways to create an art therapy job outside of the traditional hospital or group home setting. As I said when I was first introducing myself to Emery, I know that, with the right tools and guidance, I can achieve anything I set my mind to doing. This was true in school and this is true today. I know that when I am looking for work I can go anywhere I desire, I have the abilities and the knowledge from my experiences to do it all, and I have this first internship experience to thank for starting me off on the right foot.

Katryn Ellis, MA Art Therapy
Head Activity Leader, My Friends Pediatric Day Healthcare Center
Mountain View, CA
Katrynellis@gmail.com

7

ETHICS

At age 29 I moved home after graduate school, and began supervision with Carol Thayer Cox. She guided me through a difficult job that didn't last long and then was there to support me as I began to develop my contract art therapy business. There were a lot of bumps and I just kept asking, "Am I really allowed to do this?"

What I noticed was, despite all the structure, rules, regulations, boards, certifications, and licenses available, there didn't seem to be much information or guidance when it came to doing what I was trying to do. My initial thought was "I must be missing something, and, if that's the case, I am going to get in trouble for doing something I shouldn't." I can't thank Carol enough for pointing out over and over again that I was doing everything I should and asking the questions I needed to.

I found a new level of understanding when I realized that I was going to miss things now and then and that I would be making mistakes. That's how we learn. The question is what you do when you make a mistake. The goal isn't to do it perfectly the first time. The goal is not only to learn from your mistakes but to embrace them so you can grow and reach even higher next time. As long as I was searching and looking for answers, it would be okay. As long as I was continually questioning myself and what I was doing, I would eventually be able to anticipate the issues arising and set things on a better path.

Emery

Ethics are guidelines that help us learn from what has happened before us. Ethical guidelines are there to help you, so embrace them and learn from them! Many professions and facilities have their own code of professional practice. Review the codes from psychology, counseling, and your specific area of expertise to get a broader point of view. Try to think about how each code applies to you and you are already acting ethically. Some information may not apply to any immediate situation, but it's good to be familiar with all of the information as you move ahead and develop your business.

Acting ethically

- Find a supervisor or create a peer supervision group. When heading into new territory, it's good to have someone as a mentor, sounding board, and professional guide to help you get started. Even if they haven't done exactly what you are doing, they'll be able to ask questions and offer advice from a professional point of view.

- In addition to relying on a supervisor, try forming a peer supervision group. With this new adventure comes some degree of isolation since you're working on your own, so why not create and extend your own network? Finding support and creating a group that gives you the interactions you would normally have from co-workers can help lighten the sense of isolation and create a space to discuss dilemmas or ethical concerns you run into.

- Have conversations about ethics on a regular basis. Bring up the ethical dilemmas that you are facing. Have a conversation and bounce around ideas on how to best deal with them. By doing this you will gain insight, see other points of view, and better approach situations in general.

- Don't be afraid to admit when you don't know something or that a topic/population is out of your range of expertise. This is part of taking responsibility for your own and your clients' safety and wellbeing. It may mean you shouldn't proceed down the avenue you were headed, or it could be that you just need some further education and/or guidance around the subject at hand before continuing. Either way, you will learn more and find new opportunities that will deepen your experience.

- Books to read:
  - Dileo, C. (2000) *Ethical thinking in music therapy*. Cherry Hill, NJ: Jeffrey Books.
  - Furman, L.R. (2013) *Ethics in art therapy: Challenging topics for a complex modality*. London: Jessica Kingsley Publishers.
  - Moon, B. (2006) *Ethical issues in art therapy*. Springfield, IL: Charles C. Thomas Publisher.
  - Taylor, K. (1995) *Ethics of caring: Honoring the web of life in our professional healing relationships*. Santa Cruz, CA: Hanford Mead Publishers, Inc.

Organizations' codes of ethics

- Health Insurance Portability and Accountability Act (HIPAA) guidelines—www.hhs.gov/ocr/privacy/index.html.

- American Psychological Association (APA)—www.apa.org/ethics/code/index.aspx.

- American Counseling Association—www.counseling.org/resources/codeofethics/TP/home/ct2.aspx.

- American Art Therapy Association (AATA)—www.arttherapy.org.

- American Art Therapy Association—www.arttherapy.org/aata-ethics.html.

- Art Therapy Credentials Board (ATCB)—www.atcb.org/code_of_professional_practice.

- American Dance Therapy Association (ADTA)—www.adta.org/resources/Documents/CODE_of_ethics1.pdf.

- American Music Therapy Association (AMTA)—www.musictherapy.org/about/ethics.

- Certification Board for Music Therapists (CBMT)—www.cbmt.org.

- National Association for Drama Therapy (NADT)—www.nadt.org/about-nadta/code-of-ethics.html.

- NY State Office of Professions, Mental Health Practitioners—www.op.nysed.gov/prof/mhp.

- International Expressive Arts Therapy Association (IEATA)—www.ieata.org/reat-ethics.html.

I had sent out letters and release forms for the clients whose art I wanted to share in supervision and photograph. At the bottom of the form was a space for comments or questions from the family. As the forms came back to me, I found many expressions of gratitude and excitement over the work I was doing with their family member. In one there was a $20 bill. When it fell into my lap, I just stared at it in surprise. My first thought was "Oh, how nice!" My next thought was "Can I accept it?" I explored this ethical dilemma with many people over the next couple weeks. Many said, "Just keep it. It's only $20 and clearly they want to support the great work you do."

As I heard people's responses, I began to better understand my hesitations in just flat out accepting it. My thoughts centered around the bigger picture. What if this were $100 or $1000? I am not a non-profit and don't have anything set up that allows me to take donations. More to the point was the fact that the facility where I saw this person paid me well and was my most supportive employer. I knew about their financial needs and the hard work they put in to what they do. Was I taking money away from them? It would have been one thing if the money had been given to the facility with the understanding it was to support the art therapy program, but instead the family had kindly sent it to me.

I don't question the family's intentions at all. They are kind, wonderful people who I know just wanted to offer their support, which I greatly appreciate even to this day. For me, the solution came naturally as I contemplated what I should do. About two weeks after getting the money, I gave John, the head of the facility, a call and explained what had happened. His response included both the statement that it's only $20 and gratitude for taking time to figure out the right thing to do and being open to talking with him about it. In the end he asked only that I make sure to use it in a way that benefited the group at his facility and again thanked me for my work. With the help of the donation, I bought supplies for a group mosaic project, so we could make some stepping stones for their garden.

When deciding if I was ready to do contract work, some of the ethical issues I considered with my supervisor included:

- Liability—How much is my responsibility towards the agency or people I'm working with? For me, I felt that if I were going into a person's house, the liability would be 100 percent mine. That felt like too much responsibility when just starting out and according to the AATA *Ethical Principles for Art Therapists* I did not yet meet the professional qualifications to follow this line of work. However, I felt that seeing clients one on one in a facility, such as an assisted living community, would be appropriate and fit my scope of knowledge as long as I was hired and paid through the facility, not by the family. No matter where you decide that boundary is for you, make sure you have your own liability insurance and that you follow the guidelines set by your professional organizations (see Chapter 2).

- Who is paying?—To me, if I were paid directly by the client, client's family, or insurance, that would mean I was in a private practice without the protection or support of a facility, so I chose to keep that level of protection by working only with facilities that hired me and paid me directly. If they wanted to offer my services as a one-to-one art therapist and have the families pay extra, that was fine, but that was between the families and the facility. I was paid our previously agreed rate.

- Comfort level—Most importantly, continue questioning any dilemmas or uncertainties that come up for you and decide if you feel comfortable with the situation or direction things are heading. If you feel uncomfortable, either change what you're doing or stop. That's not to say stop if you feel anxious or stressed about a new group. There are always going to be clients and groups that exhaust you or just don't go well now and then, but if you feel like something is too overwhelming or outside your comfort level, that's when you might need to adjust the situation. When in doubt, discuss what is going on in supervision or with colleagues to get a new perspective.

Overall, for me, being ethically responsible came down to reading books and articles on ethical issues, talking with my supervisor about what the various ethical principles were, how that fit into what I was doing, and my intentions with my clients. Those conversations led to changing what needed to be changed or stopping actions that pushed too hard against ethical boundaries.

Ethics and specific populations

When working with people who have any type of diagnosis that can affect their mental capacity, it is highly important to understand the ethics around topics such as confidentiality, informed consent, and release forms. There are many times when the person you are working with may not be legally allowed to make certain decisions for himself or herself, or may need secondary agreement from another person before you can proceed. Always ask and never assume you know the answer. The following scenario shows how I went about attaining release forms for clients living with Alzheimer's disease. For further examination beyond this book, Furman (2013) goes more in depth and has a beautiful case study to illustrate her points.

When preparing to present a paper at my first American Art Therapy Association national conference, I had to make sure to get all the release forms for the art I was including in my talk. Since I was discussing work that involved my clients who have Alzheimer's disease, I knew there would be more work than just having the client sign a piece of paper, and I was right. By the time I figured out what I needed, I had several piles of paper, stamped envelopes, and many paper clips to get me through the process. Here is what I ended up with.

First, a packet for the family which included a nice letter explaining who I was, what I was doing with their family member, a little about art therapy, and why I was asking for a release form, while assuring them of my stance on confidentiality. This letter was on top of the release form that they needed to sign, and which included a space at the bottom where they could ask questions or write comments. Paper-clipped to both these pages was my business card. These papers were folded, and a pre-stamped envelope addressed to me was wrapped around them so the family could easily return the release form.

All of that was then put in a pre-stamped envelope that already had my return address on it, but left the space open for the facility to address the envelope to the family. This was necessary, since many of my facilities would allow me to see client records but not family addresses.

For each facility, I had a large, sturdy legal-size envelope that I would fill with as many aforementioned packets as there were participants in the art therapy program. I always made sure to leave at least one packet unsealed so the facility could see what I was sending the family members. With the packets, I also wrote a nice letter to my facility contact explaining what I was doing, saying, and expecting.

In the end, I received over 85 percent of the release forms back, and I believe the organization of the papers helped achieve that level of response. It always pays to write a nice letter and make sure what you are asking for is clear and well laid out. The simpler it is and the easier it is to send back, the more likely you will be to get a high rate of return.

Confidentiality and Ethical Considerations in the Digital Age

There are ever evolving ways to send and receive information. It is so important to remember that first and foremost a client's confidentiality must be protected and that it is very easy to unknowingly share information in an unsecured way.

How would you respond to these scenarios?

A client draws a beautiful picture of herself and her deceased husband and tells the therapist how in love they were and how much she misses him. The therapist takes a picture with her cell phone thinking she would like to include it in her file. Later that night she's online and sees a board where people have posted images for Valentine's day with the caption "True Love" and she thinks that the client's art would be perfect to share.

After a long day, two art therapy students are texting on the train ride home and discussing the challenges of their respective internship sites. One asks the other for advice on a particular client and messages a picture that shows the art the intern made while copying a client's piece of work.

A therapist can't meet her supervisor on a given day because she is out of town visiting family. They agree to Skype so as not to miss the appointment. The therapist explains to her parents that she will be back in an hour and needs to use the home office for a call. She closes the door and has the session with her supervisor during which they discuss client information and she shares artwork made by the client's.

What are some of the issues that arise for you as you read these? What would you do differently? How should the people in the situations have addressed issues as they came up? If you were the supervisor of any of these therapists what would you suggest they do next time?

It has become harder to know what is right and wrong when trying to keep up with advancements in ways of working and communicating, but there are a few simple things to remember that will help. Unless you have a signed informed consent form from your client or client's proxy that specifically says you are allowed to do something you can not do it. If you have permission to share with one person do not assume you can stretch that to include others without getting a new consent form signed. Never share client information through tweeting, posting things on social networks, or sharing on an unsecured email account. Even if the mode of communication is secure do not share it while sitting in a coffee house or anywhere public where others may overhear or see what you are doing.

As self-employed individuals you have an obligation to be very strict with yourself about how and when you share information. If in doubt always ask a supervisor and don't proceed until you are sure you understand that it is safe and secure. Our clients count on us and we have to hold ourselves to the highest standard.

Throughout the book I have included various information about ethics and how to proceed in an aware and informed manner. Now it is your responsibility to take that and apply it to your life and the situations you come across. The easiest way to know you are doing the right thing is to read the books, read the articles, do the research, and ask questions. The questions you dread asking or the moments you are least confident about are the ones you need to discuss and examine closely. For more information on ethics and electronic transmission please read Furman's (2013) book. She has extensive knowledge and a well-rounded viewpoint on this topic.

8

IT'S ABOUT THE JOURNEY

Throughout the job changes, moving, and book writing, I have learned an incredible amount about myself both personally and professionally. This book started as the notes and thoughts I wrote down when I first began contracting. It continued to develop as I supervised interns and then moved out of state. Even then I wasn't sure it would ever achieve book form. As I told friends and colleagues about contracting, I heard a lot of interest and confusion. For some, the confusion was holding them back, and I realized it would be immensely helpful for anyone interested in pursuing this line of work to have everything written down. My piecemeal advice was helpful but not as effective as a book could be.

At this point I assumed I would write something and eventually self-publish it, so those interested could buy it. I was fortunate enough to speak with someone at an AATA conference in 2010 about my book, and, as I had thought, he said it sounded interesting but that I really needed to write it before a publishing company would be interested. I began to write and pull all my notes and bits of knowledge together. When my life was flipped upside down in 2012, my book really began to form. It was something concrete I could focus on and use as an outlet. At the AATA conference in the summer of 2012, I once again spoke to the same Jessica Kingsley Publishers (JKP) representative and this time was able to show him the almost finished book. He immediately suggested I return the following day to meet Lisa Clark, senior commissioning editor with JKP.

After a brief but productive conversation, I left with her card and email address. I sent her my manuscript and six weeks later heard good news. JKP was interested. The rest is history and, assuming nothing got messed up after my manuscript was accepted, this book was published on or around April 15, 2013.

Emery

Your journey

This is your journey, so have fun and keep track of what you're doing! You will learn as you go, and there are some things you'll forget along the way or set aside to try again later. For me, some of those things I set aside never resurfaced until I looked back over my notes from a couple of years ago. I'm glad I wrote them down and have been able to revitalize my work with some of my original ideas now that I have the base on which to build. You will be your own best inspiration, so put those dreams, curiosities, and musings somewhere to find when you need them!

Projects/interventions binder

Write down what you're doing with your clients. It's great to have all of this in one place so you can go back through projects to get ideas or branch out in new directions. Flipping through your notes also gives you a sense of the variety and multifaceted approach you can take with your clients. Start with a quarter-inch binder and let your material grow naturally. As you create examples or gather releases from clients, you can add pictures of the art created from each project. This will inspire you, be a way to show prospective employers/clients what you do, and will help you document your ideas. If you have interns or colleagues, this binder can be a great reference for them as well. You can always encourage interns to add to it as they develop projects while working with you. Who knows? Maybe you'll want to publish one day!

Some questions to answer when writing up your projects:

- What materials do you need? In what quantities?
- List the basic steps you follow. What are some variations you have used or thought of?
- What has worked for you and what hasn't?
- Have you approached this project from different directions? How?
- Why and how do you adapt your projects for different people?
- Do you have some ideas for what you would like to try in the future?
- Any additional notes for someone new trying this project?

(See examples in Appendix B.)

Articles

Part of doing your best work is keeping up with what's going on in research and in your areas of expertise. When I have interns, I have them bring in articles every couple months that they find relevant to the work we are doing. I supplement that with information from the journals and publications I get on a regular basis. By the end of the year there is a good collection of articles on multiple topics that are all applicable in some way to our work. Keeping them together creates a great resource. I have used it to help friends, pull together information to speak at national conferences, educate families and staff members, and teach classes.

Operations manual

As you start this adventure, write down questions, thoughts, problems or issues you run into, ways you solve dilemmas, how you self-care, what happens when you don't take care of yourself, who you can rely on when needed, and what helps as you work through this process.

Why do this?

- It shows your progress.

- It helps prevent repeat mistakes.

- It reminds you what helps when working through difficult problems.

- It can be used as a guide for others.

- It offers reminders when you need them.

- It gives new insights into issues you face on a regular basis.

Having the information in your own words is a strong reminder of where you came from and how much you have learned.

The innovative paths of trailblazers
FAITH—MUSIC THERAPY

My professional path has been circuitous and largely self-created since graduating in 2007 from the Transpersonal Counseling Psychology Music Therapy program at Naropa University, where Emery and I were classmates. The positions in which I have worked over the last five years have been created largely from my desire to provide people of all ages and abilities with opportunities to experience an enhanced sense of self and wellness through engaging with music.

Most recently, I've been working as a hospice music therapist with a start-up hospice company serving the Metro Denver area. During my time with this company, I have been able to develop a music therapy program which has now expanded to having two music therapists on staff as part-time, hourly employees. Looking into the future, there has also been discussion about the possibility of expanding to include an internship site for music therapy students as we grow.

In addition to my work with the hospice, I teach piano and voice lessons to school-aged students at one of the local music stores, and I have had a few private psychotherapy clients. As well, I've recently partnered with a team of allied healthcare practitioners through an area non-profit organization whose mission it is to provide veterans and their families with healthcare services to which they may not otherwise have access. I also volunteer by serving on my state music therapy association as co-chair and social media representative.

While this arrangement has been stable and consistent for the last two years, these opportunities didn't come right away—it took me almost three years after graduating and obtaining my MT-BC credential before I was able to work as a recognized music therapist. During that time, I did a lot of networking and learning about organizations in the area that held similar missions and visions as my own. In terms of employment, for the two-and-a-half years prior to receiving the wonderful opportunity to work with my current hospice company, I worked in early childhood education settings for one of the area public school districts as a special education paraeducator.

Even though it can feel overly busy and full at times (not to mention the mental shifting required to work how I presently do), I enjoy my current employment arrangement. There is a certain stability I appreciate that comes from working with an established company, but because I work part-time as an hourly employee, I also have the time and space for creating or engaging in professional projects in areas of interest outside of end-of-life care and palliative medicine.

Additionally, I find it beneficial to be involved in my state's music therapy association because professional community is important to me, and I want to help make the world a better place by playing a part in the increased growth and accessibility of music therapy.

By resonating with what you ultimately desire at a core level, you create the opportunities needed for manifesting those desires.

Faith Halverson-Ramos, MA, MT-BC
Neurologic Music Therapist
www.faithhalversonramos.com
www.soundwellmusictherapy.com
http://avfinfo.org

▒ SARA—ART THERAPY

After graduating with my Art Therapy and Counseling degree, I started to work full-time in non-profits in the Chicago and surrounding area where I still live and work. Eventually, I decided that it was time to arrange my schedule in a way that felt more natural to me, namely, not 9 a.m. to 5 p.m., five days a week in an office building. I contacted Emery and, with her support and guidance, I was able to establish a few stable 6–8 hour days as a contractor with my previous full-time employer. That stable base allowed me to expand my work and develop contracts with local rehabilitation centers, other community-based mental health treatment centers, community-based studios, special recreation associations, and I have also recently started working in private practice.

The focus of my work has primarily been a strengths-based, empowerment approach to provide support for individuals and families facing physical injury, illness, chronic pain, or disability, including dementia and traumatic brain injury. The wonderful thing about working in multiple settings is that I find new inspiration every day. The variety opens and widens my perspective about my work and my approach to the people I serve. I am regularly faced with new challenges and have the time to learn new skills and expand into other areas of practice, always discovering something new and exciting, which is really important for me.

There are many challenges to working for yourself contractually and in private practice. In the beginning, money seems to come in fits and starts. It is either feast or famine. I think it is a good idea to save at least two months of expenses before you get started so you don't feel panicked when contracts cancel or individual clients don't show up for session. I once heard another self-employed therapist say, "The business part is the biggest part of a therapy business." If you are the type of person who enjoys spreadsheets and counting receipts, that will play in your favor. There are a lot of details to account for— taxes, insurance, travel costs, start-up costs, etc.—for all of which Emery was an important guide. I would definitely recommend finding a supervisor, mentor, or consultant like Emery to help with some of these detailed parts of starting a business. You don't need to reinvent the wheel, and it can be scary taking the big leap into being your own boss. Having a support system including a good cheerleader is vital.

The best advice I can give is to follow your intuition. If you have a drive to try working for yourself, you are probably the right kind of person to do it. If you've bought this book, you're probably the kind of person who will buy the rest of the "right" kind of books and talk to the right people to get you on the path that will work for you. Just take it one step at a time.

Sara M. Miller, LCPC, ATR
Art Therapist/Counselor
sarammiller@gmail.com
www.abilityarts.com

DANCING SOLO—THE TWISTS AND TURNS OF A DANCE/ MOVEMENT THERAPY PRIVATE PRACTICE

Good Fruit Expressive Arts Counseling and Psychotherapy LLC evolved as a part-time private practice in 2005 when I rented a small office space in Wilmington, Delaware. At that time I primarily saw clients in the evening and on the weekend due to my full-time work and doctoral studies schedule. Things seemed to be cruising along until mid-year 2011 when I was laid off from my full-time dance/movement therapy position. This turned out to be a blessing in disguise as I transitioned into full-time private practice and my client caseload drastically increased.

Being self-employed in private practice is an evolutionary process to meet the growing demands of the clients in the geographic location where one practices, while building a brand and unique niche that stands out from other practitioners. I initially worked with adults in individual and couples therapy who had difficulty managing stress, controlling anger, and regulating their mood. Currently, my primary specialization is helping social service professionals to develop creative expressive stress management systems so that they can avoid burnout, increase productivity, and attain life balance and peace of mind. My services include creative arts therapy (dance/movement, art, expressive writing, sandtray therapy), counseling, psychotherapy, coaching, speaking (keynote, conference, workshop), and corporate consulting.

While I greatly enjoy my work, there are many challenges and rewards to being a self-employed creative arts therapist. My skills and training as a board-certified dance/movement therapist affords me the opportunity to utilize observational assessments to recommend to my clients new expressive ways of being in the world. There is immediate gratification for me in seeing my clients reach a breakthrough by tapping into their innate creative expressions through mind/body/spirit dance/movement therapy techniques. Other rewards include defining how and when I work and with whom, in terms of individual sessions, group sessions, or contractually. Some challenges to self-employment in the creative arts therapies are attaining contracts, receiving third-party insurance reimbursement, and administrative overheads (marketing, accounting, stocking supplies, maintaining client files, etc.).

I encourage anyone who is interested in pursuing self-employment as a dance/movement therapist to recognize and respect the value of your work because others may not, make each encounter with clients and business prospects a movement experience, and optimize brand management through multiple means.

Angela Tatum Fairfax, PhD, LPC, BC-DMT, NCC
Good Fruit Expressive Arts Counselling and Psychotherapy LLC
"Express your stress, improve your health, increase your success!"
angela@goodfruitexpressivearts.com
www.goodfruitexpressivearts.com

NATALIE—MUSIC THERAPY

It is incredibly difficult to pigeonhole my work into one area. My company provides music therapy services to the midlands region of South Carolina, but the scope of who I provide services to is limited only by what I and my subcontractors can ethically address within our scopes of practice. The bulk of my work is with children with special needs, but I also provide services to adults with Alzheimer's and related dementias, people at the end of life, and children and adolescents with psychiatric or addiction concerns.

I think of starting my business as both the smartest and dumbest decision that I have ever made in my life. It is the smartest because I have never been more fulfilled by work. Everything that I do is my own, and that ownership of it lends me to take even more pride in it than I did before. I live or die by my own dedication and effort, and that is the kind of life I enjoy leading. It was the dumbest decision I ever made because I stepped off a metaphorical cliff by quitting my full-time job and diving straight into trying to create a full-time private practice. It doesn't quite work that way.

I started my private practice because there was nearly zero access to outpatient music therapy in my community. I was working in an inpatient environment, and while I loved the work that I did there and the progress that was made, I observed that regression and readmission were staples for the children and adolescents that I worked with. I wanted to be able to offer my services to these children in their environment, and so my business was founded. My long-term goal for my business is to reach a point of sustainability in which

I can offer free or reduced-cost services to the children who are unable to access music therapy through other avenues.

As of this writing, I've been in practice for over two years. I haven't yet reached my goal of providing services, but, as my business grows, I get closer to achieving it. There are certainly a lot of challenges that come with running a private music therapy practice, but I would never trade it in. Having complete ownership and pride over what I accomplish, and the knowledge that I built it from nothing, is more rewarding than a steady paycheck. Knowing the smiles and growth that my work instigates wouldn't exist if I hadn't taken the initiative to start my business is more rewarding than having a retirement plan from the get-go.

For those who are considering starting their own practice in music therapy, or any other creative arts, I have one piece of advice: find a mentor. Find ten mentors. Other therapists are doing this every day and there is no need to reinvent the wheel on basic business practice. Finding a mentor decreases the feeling of isolation, increases your creativity when it does come to running your business, and gives you a solid group of people to bounce ideas off of, rant to, and share your successes with.

We all need our own cheerleaders.

Natalie Mullis, MT-BC
Owner, Key Changes Music Therapy Services LLC
www.keychangesmusictherapy.com

JULIANNE—ART THERAPY

I have an active private practice in the Boston area, working primarily with adolescents, adults, and older adults. I focus on wellness, life transitions, issues of gender and identity, grief and loss, depression and anxiety, and those who have dementia. Recently, I have begun research and work with Beth Israel Deaconess Hospital, using art therapy with people who experience migraines. My hope is to expand that work to include people who have chronic pain. The arts are the core of my strengths-based relational approach with clients. I run individual and group supervision for students and professionals, and outside supervision for agencies with expressive therapy interns and expressive therapists. Here in Massachusetts, many art therapists are also licensed mental health counselors and we need dual continuing education credits. I have developed and run 4–6 authorized continuing education art-based workshops per year. Teaching in Lesley University's Expressive Therapies program rounds out my full-time work.

I decided to open a private practice after many years' working in a variety of agencies, most of which were based in the medical model. I was becoming increasingly dissatisfied with working from a pathology-based perspective. The universe offered me the opportunity (or kick in the pants!) when not only the older adult program I was working in unexpectedly closed but the hospital that housed the program also closed.

The rewards of the work revolve around how privileged I feel having time to accompany people on a piece of their journey(s), watching those who can do so use the arts expressively to develop strengths and find more clarity and satisfaction in their lives. For others, it is an honor for me to share positive emotional moments as their lives are ending. I so strongly believe in what we do that I love teaching others how to develop their individual identities as art therapists. Working with such a variety of people helps me remain spontaneous and creative in my approach to art therapy, my art, and my life.

Of course, there are challenges. One benefit—flexible scheduling—is also a challenge. Clients will cancel or need to reschedule, which means you have to be able to tolerate some inconsistency of your time. That can then result in a changing income. To be in private practice, you have to accept that you won't get a regular paycheck every two weeks. Unfortunately, our current tax and benefits systems penalize individuals who work independently rather than support them. Medical insurance and tax rates are higher when you are self-employed.

I think one of the most daunting challenges for many individual practitioners is marketing your business. Sometimes it is difficult for art therapists to embrace the business side of private practice. We do this work to help people, not to sell ourselves. In a previous lifetime, I was in sales management, so I have skills in this area and I know how important marketing is for the growth and success of a practice.

The work we do is difficult and complex. It is so helpful to work with a team developing understanding and treatment of clients. When in private practice, you have to create that team support. I have three words: supervision, supervision, supervision. Start a supervision group, meet regularly with a peer, or work with a mentor you respect. Make sure you maintain a regular art-making practice.

My advice if you want to begin private practice is to be prepared. Besides making sure you are the kind of person who can thrive with the ups and downs, do your "nuts and bolts" homework. What are the laws in your area? How many clients will you need to meet expenses and make a living? What is the need in the community?

Most important, build on your strengths and work from your passion.

Julianne Hertz, ATR-BC, LMHC
Art Therapist and Licensed Mental Health Counselor
www.innerarttherapy.com
artprof@comcast.net

▆ AUDREY—ART THERAPY

I graduated from the George Washington University in 2010 with my Masters in Art Therapy. Soon after my official graduation, I headed back to Ohio (where I am originally from) to begin my art therapy career. Art therapy in DC area was booming, so when I moved to central Ohio I was a bit surprised by the lack of opportunity. With a year or so of hospice experience under my belt from internships, I began volunteering at several hospices around the area. I figured this was a great way to network and gain hours towards my ATR. I was able to contribute to bereavement support groups and worked with some elderly patients, but no referrals were leading me to work with children (my target population).

I soon found that employment opportunities were few and far between in central Ohio. After months of searching for jobs without success, I was forced to look into alternatives, anxious to find a paying position. I frequented all the social networking sites, including the Art Therapy Alliance (where I eventually met Emery) and the Buckeye Art Therapy Association's website. Just as I was feeling defeated, I received a call from a hospice social worker who had a friend in need of my services. This friend had two young children grieving the loss of their father. The children were not verbal about the loss and the mother was interested in using art therapy as a tool for processing their grief. I was ecstatic that the social worker had contacted me and I was more than happy to travel to their home to conduct art therapy sessions, but what was the next step? This would be a paying gig and a territory I knew nothing about. I was very unaware of the "business" side of things with contract art therapy and self-employment. These were things that coursework never taught me, and I felt the need for an advisor. I began seeing my ATR-BC supervisor at this time and we discussed ATCB regulations in detail to determine what rules needed to be followed. After creating my own contract for art therapy services, gaining detailed advice from Emery, and putting together an approved artwork release form, I began visiting with my new clients weekly.

As time went on, I gained another client and a full-time position at a hospice where I was able to use art therapy as a secondary title. I really enjoyed working with my clients but have decided to focus on my full-time position for the time being.

I continue to advocate for art therapy amidst the hospice population and cannot wait to read up on all the new information and advice Emery has put together for this book! I know others are struggling, and I believe that contract work can open many doors for us. Speaking as a new professional, this book is a necessity for a time when art therapy jobs are sparse and art therapists are required to market themselves and their services to a population of companies that may not understand the product we offer. I hope this book inspires confidence and a proactive outlook to those facing similar struggles.

My advice would be: learn to market yourself, know and believe that what you have to offer is desirable and essential to the wellbeing of others.

Audrey Evans, MA
Art Therapist
Columbus, OH
a-evans@live.com

MY NON-LINEAR JOURNEY AS AN ARTIST ENTREPRENEUR

As early as I can remember, I knew that I wanted to be an artist. My father, who had survived the Holocaust and seen the starving artists in Paris, would say, "Artist shmartist—be a teacher."

Little did I know that one day I would be both—and with a PhD no less.

Like many of us creatives, my path has not been linear. I lived the bohemian poverty life for a long time until one day I realized that I couldn't keep struggling that way.

Prior to this, I had been lucky enough to fall into illustrating and writing children's picture books through an exhibition of raw and bloody art that I'd had. My work, although intensely therapeutic, has always been narrative and colorful, even when dealing with things like my parents' deaths, the Holocaust, and my Jewishness in paintings.

Making children's books taught me that it "never is too late to have a happy childhood," and it was through these books that I began teaching both children and adults. The books also helped me get accepted into a prestigious art program to do an MFA. And while the royalties from my books did provide sushi, new shoes, the occasional big vacation, and other goodies twice a year, it wasn't enough to live on.

After completing my MFA, I continued teaching but also started teaching in colleges as well. Financially, it was still a struggle, except for those magical moments when royalty checks came in. So when I was invited to do a PhD (through the books again), I decided: maybe I'll have financial security and be a university professor.

Although it was incredibly hard learning to think more analytically, I loved the intellectual stimulus and the process of learning at such a high level. After I graduated, I ended up working in a department in the Midwest where I did not fit in. I discovered that being a university professor was not for me and after three years I quit my job and moved back to Northern California.

By then I had become interested in working with seniors and trained in this work through the Alzheimer's Association. I also attended an art therapy conference where I met Emery who also mentored me in this process. My first time working with seniors was a disaster, but with time and experience it got better and better and now I love it. I see it as a spiritual practice going in with an open heart and an open mind.

At some point, I realized I also wanted to engage with a wider range of ages and use my PhD work teaching "how to" courses with meaning. I knew I didn't want to teach in institutions anymore, and I also knew that I now had the qualifications, experience, and organizational skills to start my own school—so I did. After much work, I launched the Picture Book Academy where I now teach innovative interactive online courses in art, mythology, and personal growth, as well as courses in writing, and illustrating, children's picture books. So far they've been a huge success, where I'm known as a life changer because of the transformative nature of my work. I love my students and seniors and feel fortunate, fulfilled, and very happy.

If you are curious about my work, please come visit www.picture bookacademy.com or my personal site at www.mirareisberg.com. One of my courses might be just what you are looking for.

Mira Reisberg
Director of the Picture Book Academy
miraguy@gmail.com
www.picturebookacademy.com

CRISTA—ART THERAPY

I worked as an art therapist at a psychiatric hospital in the DC area known for admitting referrals from the US Secret Service. After a colorful and intense experience, it was time to move on after my department was disbanded and its employees' responsibilities changed drastically. As I explored opportunities to apply my art therapy skills, I heard about contracting as a form of employment from my graduate school job board. I met Emery and we discussed the pros and cons of contracting. I was inspired to give this approach a try in part due to Emery's level-headedness, enthusiasm, and willingness to be a mentor. I also knew I would be starting a family soon, so an opportunity that afforded flexibility in schedule combined with variability in clientele and freedom to select the work and environment really appealed to me.

The resulting full-time schedule was composed of a part-time art therapy job with a non-profit organization, in-home art therapy with another organization, and my contract work with various facilities. I am still taking care of my child, so I've chosen to continue only the contract art therapy groups in Northern Virginia with facilities that include assisted living residences and an Alzheimer's day center. Acquiring contracting work required marketing my services to the activities director of the facilities and educating the decision makers about the value of art therapy and its beneficial impact on the participants.

My goal is to offer seniors in these facilities an artistic outlet, whether they are living with dementia and Alzheimer's or independently in a senior residence. The focus of most of my groups is to encourage each participant's individual expression. I provide an environment and artistic opportunity for independent expression, regardless of how small or big that may be or how slow or brief the process may be.

I find that honoring participants' individual expressions is both the most rewarding and most challenging aspect of the art therapy groups. I focus on the participants' strengths, but I also remind staff that it's important for participants to have opportunities to use their strengths in art to express any emotion; to use that non-verbal outlet not only to express joyful memories but also to communicate fear or anxiety. Being a contractor makes me an automatic outsider to the hosting organization: I'm a guest in the environment with established norms and expectations. On the one hand, this can make my art therapy groups an exciting addition to the facility, and, on the other hand, my approach can be different from the facilities' routine activities and need further introduction. Most often, the facilities appreciate the perspective I bring and the communication and expression that art therapy elicits from their clients.

As an outside contractor, I am better able to concentrate solely on the clients and less likely to become entangled in the dynamics within the facility. I primarily see the clients only in the art therapy groups; therefore, despite taking longer to get to know them, I often get to see them in a more capable and positive light. On a few occasions I assisted my clients with projects not related to art therapy. This interaction helped me better understand the operating environment and organizational dynamics.

It's all about the people. Art therapy enables participants to create art that communicates something in their minds. More facilities need to offer art therapy groups to their residents to support them in living their lives.

Crista L. Kostenko, ATR-BC
Board-certified and registered Art Therapist
zateshno@gmail.com
www.artstateofmind.com

SARAH—MUSIC THERAPY

I never pictured myself as the business owner that I am today. I switched majors to study music therapy because I really wanted to help others and to be happy in my job. When I finished my internship, I was not able to move because of my family circumstances and there were no full-time music therapy jobs in my city. I had to create my own job. I often worked three part-time jobs while trying to build my practice. They say that it takes 3–5 years to really build a business, but it took me longer than that. I had a few bumps in my personal life along the way, and chose to pursue a graduate degree as well. Ultimately, relocation to Denver, Colorado, was key to building my business success.

My business recently expanded to include two employees. We provide individual and group neurologic music therapy services to individuals with developmental disabilities and to individuals with neurologic diseases, injuries, and disorders. We contract with facilities such as hospitals, adult day facilities, and senior living facilities. We provide individual sessions in our clinic and in clients' homes.

Creating my business has been much more difficult than I would have imagined, but it has also been far more rewarding than I could have imagined. There are moments I get to share with clients that are incredibly touching. They are unforgettable, break-through moments that there are no words to describe. Not only have I been able to leave a trail of lives changed for the better, but I have also been able to create opportunity for other music therapists to do the same.

Sarah Thompson, MM, MT-BC, CBIS
Neurologic Music Therapist-Fellow
Sarah@RRMusicTherapy.com
www.RRMusicTherapy.com

CREATIVE WELLBEING WORKSHOPS, LLC

We started providing workshops after we had been training art therapists and mental health professionals about positive psychology, "the science of wellbeing" (based upon the premise that the relief of suffering does not necessarily lead to happiness and that wellbeing emerges as much from focusing on strengths as trying to correct weakness). During one of our presentations, an art therapist who had become a law enforcement officer urged us to do a workshop at her agency. She felt that her fellow officers had become so burnt-out that they had lost sight of the strengths that had brought them to their work. We realized that we wanted to reach out more to "frontline providers"—police officers, hospital workers, mental health providers—and help them reconnect with the values and passion that initially moved them to choose their field. That inspired us to create a service in which we provided organizations with on-site workshops blending positive psychology principles with arts-based interventions designed to reduce burnout and stress and increase wellbeing, vitality, and engagement.

We created a concise "menu" of workshops from which organizations can choose (e.g. Drawing Strengths: Identifying and Developing Our Highest Potential; Bouncing Forward: Creatively Dealing with Adversity; and arts-based creativity workshops such as Gratitude Art Journaling, Altered Books, Mandalas for Centering). The menu helped us develop content that we could easily repeat (with minor tweaking based upon the needs that the organization provides). We offer a discount for booking a "package" of multiple workshops.

We also provide supervision and consultation, and we see clients individually. Many of our referrals come from the workshops we have provided. We market ourselves by providing free lectures in the community and by networking with other service providers (both within and outside of mental health). We found it helpful to hire a business coach to help us articulate our business objectives, and we also utilize resources such as the Creative Entrepreneur, social media, networking groups, and the local small business development organizations (www.sba.gov/content/small-business-development-centers-sbdcs). It has also been critical to build a professional online presence.

Because we knew that it might take a couple of years for us to become profitable, we focused first on getting our name out there, collaborating with others, and establishing ourselves in the art therapy community and the broader mental health community.

The greatest lessons we have learned were the following. Clarify your mission and vision: it will help sustain you while you experiment with different approaches to marketing and getting clients. Become a resource to others and your community—be less attached to getting customers than to educating and empowering others. Develop relationships not clients. Think of what your ideal practice would be like in the future and work back from there. If you work with partners, think highly of them and capitalize on the strengths you each bring.

Creative Wellbeing Workshops LLC, founded by Rebecca Wilkinson, MA, ATR-BC, and Gioia Chilton, MA, ATR-BC, provides workshops, consulting, and support to individuals and organizations experiencing high levels of stress. We are based in DC and provide services on-site throughout the country.

Creative Wellbeing Workshops LLC
Rebecca Wilkinson, MA, ATR-BC
Gioia Chilton, MA, ATR-BC
Washington, DC
Rebecca@creativewellbeingworkshops.com
www.creativewellbeingworkshops.com

▓ DONNA—DANCE/MOVEMENT THERAPY

I have worked as a dance/movement therapist with people of all ages and range of abilities/challenges for more than 30 years. For the past ten years I have focused on working with people with dementia, especially mid- to late-stage, because at this stage in my career I find this work the most satisfying. While most people know that people with dementia are responsive to music, few people understand how much people with significant dementia can and ought to move. Because inability to initiate is one symptom of dementia, they need to be invited by experienced dance/movement practitioners so that they can experience a greater sense of vitality.

It was in working with people with considerable cognitive deficits and physical disabilities who were behaviorally challenging for staff, and difficult for me to engage in groups, that I created a product called the Octaband®. Finding that the Octaband® was hugely successful in engaging people with all levels of dementia, I began to manufacture and market it. Since that time, the Octaband® has been selling to service providers who run groups for people across the spectrum of ages and abilities, locally and around the world.

For the past six years the Octaband® has become my three-dimensional business card—my mandala as it were—which visually manifests my vision of a world where people of diverse abilities can come together to play, feel good about their individual contributions, and experience a sense of belonging within a group.

In addition to selling the Octaband®, I provide direct dance/movement therapy group services, mostly locally in the Boston area, in a number of assisted livings, elderly housing, and nursing homes. As an advocate for people with dementia, in an attempt to improve their quality of life and the environments in which they live, I offer two trainings nationally to caregivers: first, Bringing Dance to People with Dementia™; and second, an Embodied Approach to Nonverbal Communication Training.

I present at conferences locally and nationally, hoping to inspire others to work with people with dementia because they desperately need us. I am currently in the process of filing for non-profit status so that my business can apply for grants, thus expanding my reach and providing research possibilities for dance/movement therapists working with this population. I also teach as adjunct faculty for Lesley University's dance therapy specialization and supervise dance therapists towards their certification and beyond.

As a creative arts therapist, one of my greatest challenges is seeing beyond the cultural paradigm which seems to say that if one is providing a service, one needn't be paid well. I am very grateful to and highly recommend the business coaches at SCORE (non-profit branch of the SBA) who provide free consultations from retired executives. With their help, I can see clearly that I am offering significant expertise and a service that is not sufficiently recognized. I believe that I/we should be well paid. We are pioneers; we need to believe in ourselves and the value that we provide. As we do, others will be willing to pay us to care for their parents, their children, their loved ones.

Donna Newman-Bluestein, Med. BC-DMT, LMHC
Dance for Connection "to self, others, and the world around"
www.dancetherapymusings.com
donna@octaband.com
Octaband LLC
www.octaband.com

▮ CATHERINE—ART THERAPY

When I arrived at Saturday's assisted living facility and found the activity room under construction, I was not entirely sure how the day's art therapy session would go. The activities coordinator directed me to the end of the second-floor hallway, where a couch and two folding chairs were arranged around a coffee table. Again, I was not sure how the session would go, but at least we had chairs. With five years under my belt as an art therapist and four of those years spent contracting, I have worked in a variety of settings, some more traditional than others. From activity rooms to hallways, gymnasiums, and even beauty parlors, I am no longer surprised by the locations I find myself practicing art therapy in.

It is in our training, our experience, and our very nature to be creative in how we relate to our clients, so it's not surprising we also have to be creative in where we find our work. Prior to this, I lived in Washington, DC, where I attended graduate school and worked for my first year as an art therapist in a "regular" full-time position. I was eager and excited to experience big city living, but, even at the time, I knew my ultimate goal was to bring art therapy back to the South, to an area where the need was great but the profession under-utilized. With inspiration from this book's author and, as always, the mysterious inner workings of fate, I found myself living below the Mason-Dixon Line a lot sooner than I had expected.

As my brother frankly stated, "You'll be able to corner the market." In some ways, he was right. With few or no art therapists in the area, I was sure to have next to nothing in the way of competition. While there were no art therapists to compete with, there were also no art therapy jobs. I knew even before I moved that I would have to be the one to create those jobs. And I did. I started with a handful of contracts with assisted living facilities and dementia day care centers in my first year. I was able to establish a presence, make connections, and within three years' time create relationships with over 25 different organizations in my area.

While contracting in its very nature provides the freedom to conduct your work in your own way, there are a few points I found essential to starting a practice and helping that practice grow:

Marketing

Words cannot express how important it is to have a web presence when starting any business, but especially an art therapy practice. (If only I could paint you a picture!) I have used all kinds of marketing materials in my work: mailers, brochures, business cards. All of these are helpful, but none comes close to the stimulating visual testament of a well-made website.

Networking

Tell everyone you meet about what you do. You never know who will know someone who knows someone who needs an art therapist. I landed my first contract through the childhood friend of my college roommate's mother, who just happened to work for an organization looking for an art therapist. Professional networking groups can be helpful in this regard as well. There may not be local art therapy associations where you work, but I guarantee there are professional groups based around the population you work with. I owe my current work to speaking at such a group.

Focus your population

Keep your client population narrow in scope when starting your practice. It can and will be overwhelming to advertise and market to multiple groups. Placing your focus on one group will make you the expert in your field, in your region, and, most importantly, for your clients. This helps to keep things simple (and you sane) in the beginning. Subsequently, opportunities to work with other populations will come up along the way as word spreads and people begin to hear about the amazing things you are doing with your clients.

Be creative

We are not traditional talk therapists by any means. We are so much more. So it should stand that we do not always work in the most traditional of settings. I began with assisted living facilities, but then found work with two art museums whose education departments were progressive enough to realize they could use their extensive resources to bring art therapy to a wide range of populations and to do so in a unique and beautiful setting as well.

Payment

As art therapists, we do what we do because we love and believe in the work. Most of us did not come to the field looking for large paychecks. However, we should not be afraid to charge what our services are worth. We are highly trained specialists in the mental health profession and should be respected as such. That reputation starts with how we choose to present ourselves.

I do not wish to be misleading in my description of my work and would never want to sugarcoat the realities of working as a contract art therapist. Building an art therapy practice of this nature takes a tremendous amount of work, patience, and perseverance. Yet, if you are willing to take a leap, to put in the time and effort necessary, the rewards will ultimately follow. While there have certainly been trying times of low pay, part-time retail jobs, and people who just do not understand the power of art therapy, I have never regretted my decision to fly solo. Because I have traveled my own path, I have been able to reach the patients of not just one facility but dozens. I have been able to educate not one administrator on the power and importance of art therapy but many. And perhaps most importantly, I have been able to continue the work that I love in a place that I love.

Catherine M. Harris, MA, ATR-BC
Art Therapist
cathrine@catherineharris.com
www.catherineharris.com

My journey

Throughout my life, art has been a part of what I do. I was born with amblyopia—lazy eye—so I grew up literally seeing the world differently from most people. When I had to wear a patch over my good eye to help strengthen my bad eye, my parents and I would draw with markers to decorate my patches. Art made it fun and positive. That's the part I remember; not that I had trouble seeing or that kids sometimes poked my patched eye.

FIGURE 8.1 Author and artist, Reeree, hard at work
Source: photo taken by Alison Hurst, 1979

High school and college

This interest and enjoyment in creatively exploring the world around
me continued through high school at the Madeira School and as a
directing student in the theater program at Carnegie Mellon University.
During the summers, I worked in summer stock theater and then
began working at a summer camp teaching riflery and archery. My
first time at the sleep-away camp, I was approached to instruct on the
high-flying trapeze because I had juggling on my resume. You never
know what will open the door to something new and interesting. I
said yes and continued in that role off and on over the next eight years.

Grandma

In 2002, my grandmother was diagnosed with Alzheimer's disease
after years of signs that something was changing. Following my

grandfather's death and the progression of her disease, my father found a facility that specialized in Alzheimer's care and we moved her in. It happened to be right down the street from where I was living in McLean, Virginia, at the time, so every few days I would go by and have lunch with her or just sit and chat for a while. I began bringing in some drawing supplies to give us something to do together and was amazed at how the activity drew a crowd of residents and always ended up as a small group doing art projects.

It was around this time that I was looking for my next adventure in life and I happened across art therapy. Psychology had always interested me and I had been making art my entire life, so the combination seemed natural. As I researched the topic more, I found several programs I thought would be a good fit, and they had similar prerequisites. I began taking the required psychology and visual art courses at the local community college, assuming I would either enjoy them or realize that I didn't care for this new career I was pursuing. I loved it!

As I visited Grandma, I would tell her about what I was doing and how interesting it was. She asked some great questions and our conversations were upbeat, although a bit repetitive because of her dementia. As the Alzheimer's progressed, she began having trouble recognizing people. During my visits in 2004, before I went away to graduate school, she would regale me with tales about how her granddaughter Emery was studying art therapy and how exciting it was. She thought I was remarkably similar to her granddaughter. Instead of seeing this as a sad stage in her decline, I found it heartwarming and felt lucky that these happy and positive thoughts about me and my life were what had stuck with her even as her memory was fading.

Naropa

In August of 2004, I moved to Boulder, Colorado. My brother, Jory, came with me on the drive out west to help with the move. I trusted everything would work out, but it was still scary to leave my family behind and go the furthest away from home I'd ever been for so long a period of time. The trip out was emotional, and I almost turned back that first night when we ended up in a not-so-great room at a hotel and I discovered I had lost my driver's license. Mama calmed me down and went through the practically insurmountable process of getting me a temporary license from the DMV and faxing it to me at another hotel a day or two later. I don't know if he realizes it, but Jory kept me going. He stayed solid and grounded, and learned how to drive my stickshift car the second day of the trip. Because of him I made it through the trip out to Colorado and survived without furniture in my new apartment for a few days. Although it was hard to drop him off at the airport, by the time he left I felt okay about this new path in my life and was ready to start and adjust to being on my own.

Naropa was one of the best things I have ever done. I threw myself into the program and was determined to learn everything I could about art therapy, Buddhism, meditation, and myself. I met incredible people, processed a lot of my own "stuff," and made it out the other side with a new-found confidence and understanding of both myself and the world around me. At the beginning I had made a rule that if someone asked for a volunteer, I would raise my hand before my brain kicked in to stop me. It was scary—but it worked.

While going through school, I volunteered at a retirement home and took classes at the Alzheimer's Association in Denver, still the best chapter I have ever been a part of. My interest in working with the elderly and people with Alzheimer's continued to grow and the volunteer work turned into my third-year internship. The meditation and training from Naropa helped immensely with the work I was doing with people who had memory impairment. I practiced patience and gentle guidance, while having to remain in the moment because that's where my clients with dementia always were. It became important to keep the concept of basic goodness close to my heart, especially when a client was disoriented and confused or lashed out. Seeing things from the client's point of view became a practice I required of myself to better understand situations as they arose. We had tea-time after naps in the afternoon and would sip hot chocolate together and chat. I became very close with one woman, and she is one of the people who inspired me to continue this type of work after graduation. Being with her for nine months taught me so much.

The lessons I learned were rich and valuable when I took the time to slow down and just listen. It amazed me how aptly the knowledge I gained at Naropa—through meditation, contemplation, keeping a holistic viewpoint, and the transpersonal approach—paralleled and informed my work with those who have Alzheimer's. This was the right program for me.

Contract art therapy

I moved back east in May of 2007, got married in September, and started my first job as an art therapist. The job was not such a great fit, but, instead of panicking, I found support in my supervisor and after a couple of months of uncertainty I quit. My focus turned towards working with retirement homes and bringing art to people who have Alzheimer's. I had seen the need to bring the art to the people instead of vice versa for years, but hadn't known how I could help. I still didn't have any idea what I was getting into and so I began researching what it meant to be an independent contractor. For two months I researched, asked questions, and began forming a marketing packet to send to the retirement homes in the area.

In December I sent out a batch of packets that included a cover letter, resume, presentation (complete with printouts of the PowerPoint slides I had given as my final presentation at Naropa), and two articles on the benefits of art therapy. Two weeks later I followed up with phone calls. Out of the 35 packets I sent out, I received only one response a month later from an activities director. This was my first interview. I went in and we talked for half an hour, seemed to hit it off, and decided on the schedule and fee. Looking back, I was underpaid, overworked, and learned an enormous amount from this first job. It was eye-opening when, two months later, my second job interview offered me double what the first job offered. As I continued getting calls over the next couple months, I adjusted my marketing tactics and fee scale to reflect what I was learning. I changed what I sent in the packets, the types of questions I asked, the boundaries I placed on the work, and the sliding scale. With these adjustments came a better response to the mailings. The only rule I had at the beginning that still applies now is this: until I hear "no" from a site, I continue sending them information.

Years later I am still adjusting the information as I get feedback or understand the ever-varying needs of the facilities and clients. It was almost a full year before I thought of offering a free session as an interview tool. Once I did, the response rate to my packets jumped to above 50 percent. Since I started this process in 2007, I have gone through the entire organizational process in metropolitan Washington, DC, had two interns from George Washington University, guest-lectured on transpersonal psychology and art therapy at GW, trained and handed that business over to two women before moving to Long Island, entered back into working for a facility on a part-time basis, navigated the NY state licensing process for creative arts therapists, rebuilt my contract business on Long Island as an artist and then art therapist, presented papers at two American Art Therapy Association conferences, and started consulting or mentoring others interested in starting their own contract businesses.

As I am finishing this book, I realize there are several new events from the past year that I want to include. My marriage has ended, and with that has come a lot of change. I am once again on my own, I have written and am about to have my first book published, I have opened a private practice in Huntington, NY, and I am eagerly planning to move to Brooklyn, NY, this coming summer. There have been many challenges and many rewards. Somewhere in my future I hope to establish my own wellness center, form a non-profit, meet some amazing people, and get a dog. You have to keep dreaming! I continually try to step into change and to grow from the experiences that come with it. I hope to continue the work I love with seniors and therapists for a long time and to celebrate as new areas of life are opened up for exploration. While living in the moment and being open to where this path takes me, I also can't wait to see what happens next!

Emery Hurst Mikel
emery.mikel@gmail.com
www.creativelyhealing.com

TEMPLATES AND FORMS

Resume

Street address * Brooklyn, NY 11215
Phone # * emery.mikel@gmail.com
www.creativelyhealing.com

Objective: A position developing therapeutic arts based programming for people with Alzheimer's disease and their families within a supportive, energetic environment.

SUMMARY OF QUALIFICATIONS

- 10+ years experience working with groups and individuals.
- Skilled at developing and facilitating arts-based therapeutic programming.
- Lead art therapy groups for people with Alzheimer's, developmental disabilities, aphasia, and physical limitations.
- Reliable and hard working; ability to collaborate in a team effort.
- Enthusiastic and committed to the health and wellbeing of clients.
- Train interns and guest lecture at George Washington University.
- Mentor and train professional art therapists transitioning into self-employment.

EMPLOYMENT

2013–Present   **Program Coordinator**   Alzheimer's Disease Resource Center, Bayshore, NY

- Developing and implementing the center's art program.
- Training and visiting facilitators at the 20+ facilities involved in the program.
- Organizing, hanging, and running the annual art show that is attended by participants, families, and staff.
- Developing and leading the annual facilitator training.
- Maintaining all administrative tasks associated with the program including, but not limited to, release forms, supply ordering or distribution, record keeping, spreadsheets, newsletters, certificates, matting or framing of artwork, and phone support for facilities.

2008–Present   **Contract Art Therapist**   MD, VA, DC and Long Island, NY

- Working as an independent contractor bringing art therapy to the elderly and adults in a variety of facilities.
- Developing and facilitating arts-based therapeutic programming in community centers, retirement home, and intergenerational centers.
- Lead art therapy groups for elders with dementia, cognitive impairments, and/or physical disabilities, as well as those who were more independent.

- Work on cognitive, physical, and emotional needs through drawing, painting, collage, mosaics, and quilting.
- Create a chance for non-verbal communication, reminiscence and memory recall through art making.
- Create a space where the participants have choices and power over what they create; build self-confidence and a sense of identity beyond age and diagnosis.
- Provide a sense of productivity through projects and art shows.
- Skills are practiced and self-expression is valued.
- Group discussion and input are encouraged.

CURRENT AND PAST COMPANIES

List of Companies when appropriate in terms of confidentiality and what the facility allows.

2009	Hospice Volunteer	Capital Hospice, District of Columbia
2008–10	Supervisor of Art Therapy Interns	George Washington University., District of Columbia
2005–07	Art Therapy Intern with People who have Alzheimer's	Frasier Meadows, Boulder, CO
2005–06	Mentor in Community Art Studio	Naropa University, Colorado
2003–07	Lead Teacher	Virginia, Colorado, Maryland
1997–2002	Trapeze/Indoor Circus Instructor	Camp Lohikan, Pennsylvania

PUBLICATIONS, LECTURES AND PRESENTATIONS

2013, 11, 09, 08	Guest Lecturer on Transpersonal Psychology and Art Therapy	George Washington University, DC
2013	*The Art of Business: A Guide to Self Employment for Creative Arts Therapists*	Jessica Kingsley Publishers
2012	*New Visions for Alzheimer's Care: Bringing a Studio Approach into the Community*	AATA, GA
2010	*The Secret World of the Elderly: A Studio Approach that Raises Awareness*	AATA Conference, CA
2010	*Young at Art: The Endless Possibilities of Art Therapy with Senior Adults*	(Panel) AATA Conference, CA

EDUCATION AND TRAINING

2012	Licensed Creative Arts Therapist—NY State Board of Education.
2010	Board Certified Registered Art Therapist—Art Therapy Credentials Board.
2009	Capital Hospice Patient Care Training—Washington, DC.
2007	M.A., Transpersonal Counseling Psychology: Art Therapy—Naropa University, Boulder, CO.
2006	Certificate in Dementia Care—Alzheimer's Association, Denver, CO.
2000	B.F.A., Drama: Directing—Carnegie Mellon University, Pittsburgh, PA.

Cover letter

Emery Mikel
Street address
City, state and zip code

Facility name
Attn: Programs Director
5555 Start Working Way
City, state and zip code

Art Therapy
Phone number
emery.mikel@gmail.com
www.creativelyhealing.com

Dear (Person's name or title, e.g. Programs Director),

I am currently offering a free workshop for those interested in adding art therapy to their program. I'll bring all the supplies for an hour-long painting group of up to 10 participants. No prior art experience is necessary and currently I work with independent seniors, people with developmental disabilities, and those in every stage of Alzheimer's disease or other dementias. My belief is that everyone can benefit from and enjoy the art making process and I appreciate the chance to show you what I do. After the free hour we can meet to discuss your needs and talk about what fits your budget for future groups. I'd like to draw your attention to the following points.

- Licensed in New York.
- Available weekdays and **evenings**.
- Free trial art therapy group.
- All levels of ability welcome.
- Special training and experience with dementia/Alzheimer's disease.
- Flexible schedule and sliding scale for future groups.
- Variety of programming opportunities available, including art history.

Please take a moment to look over my resume for a more in-depth explanation of my work and education. I have been a contract art therapist for several years now, and have found art can be an amazing way to work with seniors and adults. As I get to know your community, I will tailor the projects to specifically address your groups' interests and abilities. My main goal is to offer projects that can create a sense of productivity and empowerment for the participants and along the way I will add diversity through painting, quilting, collage, and book making. Whether it's painting a still life or just making one stroke with a paintbrush, art making can offer something for everyone.

After the free workshop we can discuss your needs and possible future sessions. My hours are flexible throughout the week and my hourly fee is based on a sliding scale that takes into account travel time, frequency, and group size as well as including all necessary supplies. I have found the groups derive the most benefit from the sessions when we can meet regularly, and will work around your schedule and budget to provide the best service for your community. Please call or email so we can set up a time for the free session and to discuss your needs. I'll be happy to answer any questions you might have.

Thank you for your time.

Signature
Printed name with credentials

Invoice

Invoice   #397

Emery Mikel
Street address
City, state and zip code

Facility name
Attn: Contact name/title
Street address
City, state and zip code

Art Therapy
Phone number
emery.mikel@gmail.com
www.creativelyhealing.com

ID # if needed by facility
Pay Rate: $55 an hour

Date	Description of work	# Hours	Fee
9/10/12	Art Therapy—description if needed	1	$55
9/11/12	Art Therapy—description if needed	1	$55
9/12/12	Art Therapy—description if needed	1	$55
9/24/12	Art Therapy—description if needed	1	$55
9/25/12	Art Therapy—description if needed	1	$55
		Total	$275

Signature .... Date ....

Art therapy agreement

Art Therapy Agreement or Bill of Rights

This is an agreement between Emery Mikel, Art Therapist, and .... regarding the contract art therapy services being offered at .... If at any time this agreement needs to be revised, the art therapist and facility contact will discuss the changes and sign a new form.

The art therapist agrees to:
- Arrive 5–10 minutes early in order to begin setting up.
- Create and run a .... minute group for up to .... participants.
- Provide all supplies for projects.
- Call promptly and cancel the group if ill.
- Work with facility contact to make sure dates for subsequent months are scheduled in a timely manner and give as much advance notice as possible for any conflicts that arise.
- Respond to calls and emails in a timely fashion, usually within 24 hours.
- Keep facility contact up to date as to the progress of the group and individuals in it.
- Send invoices to facility contact by the 5th of the month following the provision of services.

The Facility Contact agrees to:
- Schedule .... groups a month at a cost of .... a group.
- Provide an adequate space with tables and access to water.
- Assure staff will be in the room in case assistance is needed.
- Give at least 48 hours notice for cancellations. If between 24- and 48-hour notice, the facility will pay 50 percent of the art therapist's fee for the missed session. If under 24 hours, the facility agrees to pay 100 percent of the fee for the missed group.
- Call immediately if group needs to be canceled for anything outside the facility's control such as weather or emergencies.
- Give 1 month's notice if services are to be terminated. (a month is defined as a period of 30 days).
- If less than 1 month's notice is given, facility contact agrees to pay art therapist 50 percent of cost of canceled groups.
- Discuss any issues, concerns, or questions with the art therapist as they arise.
- Meet with art therapist every 2–3 months to discuss what is currently happening and plan for the future.

Art Therapist .... Date .... Phone # ....

Facility contact .... Date .... Phone # ....

Contract

Catherine M. Harris, MA
Art Therapist
Address goes here
Phone number
Email address

ART THERAPY CONTRACT

By entering into this contract, ... (the employer) agrees to employ Catherine M. Harris as an independent contractor for therapeutic art services, starting .... (date), as outlined by the sections below.

Professional Fees, Billing, and Payment
- The employer agrees to pay the contractor **$55** for every hour-long art therapy session administered.
- The employer will pay the contractor by cash or check on a monthly basis.
- Payment must be rendered within two weeks of the last session of the month.
- Should the employer need to cancel a scheduled session, the employer will give the contractor 24 hours' advance notice. When 24 hours or more of advance notice is given, the contractor will only charge the employer 20 percent of the agreed hourly fee for the canceled session. If 24 hours' advance noticed is not given to the contractor, the employer will be charged for the scheduled session and is expected to pay in full, unless both employer and contractor agree that cancellation is due to circumstances beyond the employer's control, such as the occurrence of inclement weather.
- Should the contractor need to cancel a scheduled session, the contractor will give the employer as much advance notice as possible and will not charge the employer for the canceled session.

Time and Date of Sessions
- The employer agrees to schedule .... (#) hour-long art therapy sessions per week, occurring on:
  - .... (day/s)
  - from .... to .... (time/s).
- Under the days and times stated above, the contractor agrees to commit .... hours a week of art therapy services to the employer.
- The first art therapy session will start on .... (date) and continue for the following .... months until .... (date).
- Should the employer choose to terminate the contractor's services without just cause before the end date noted above, the employer will agree to pay a termination fee of ....

.... Employer initials
.... Contractor initials

Art Therapy Services

- By entering into this contract, the contractor agrees to facilitate art therapy sessions for the employer's clients for 60 minutes per session.
- During these sessions, the contractor will work to the best of her ability to create a therapeutic environment in which the employer's clients can experiment with art materials, learn new artistic techniques, and express themselves both verbally through discussion and nonverbally through artwork.
- The contractor will serve as the facilitator of these sessions, leading group members in discussion, instructing group members in how to use materials, and encouraging group members in creating their own artwork.
- By entering into this contract, the employer understands the therapeutic value of art therapy sessions and will work with the contractor to provide optimal conditions for all sessions. These conditions include but are not limited to:
  - a clean, well-lit working space, free of loud noises and distractions
  - a flat surface to work on and comfortable chairs for the employer's clients
  - the provision of art materials as decided upon before the session by both the employer and the contractor
  - assistance from the employer in both identifying clients appropriate for sessions and gathering and encouraging clients to come to sessions
  - the provision of any information about the employer's clients that may help the contractor in working with the employer's clients.

Signature

We the undersigned have read this statement, understand, and agree with its terms.

.... (Employer) .... (Date)

.... (Contractor) .... (Date)

.... Employer initials
.... Contractor initials

Newsletter

Hello!

I hope his finds everyone doing well. I wanted to send out a newsletter to say thank you for everything you have all done for me over the past year. It has been almost exactly one year since I started as a vendor running my own contract art therapy business, and if it hadn't been for your trust and support, I wouldn't be here starting my second year working with 19 different facilities—a definite increase from the three facilities I went to this time last year. So thank you and I look forward to continuing to serve you and your elders. As always, please feel free to let me know about any thoughts, questions, or feedback you might have.

Since things have become so much busier, let me take a minute to tell you how everything is going and what's been happening over the past few months. We've been doing a lot of drawing and painting lately, so it's time for a shift to collage and mosaics with beans, tiles, crushed rock, and mirrors. These projects will focus on manipulation, organization, conceptualizing an image, fine motor skills and following a multi-step process. I'll work on transitioning from the skills we've been building over the past few months to the newer projects. Even when the memory of the project is gone, the skills learned can be built on in the next project.

Genevieve, my art therapy intern, has been doing an excellent job and is currently running three groups at various sites on her own as well as working with an individual. She's learned a lot and added valuable energy and inspiration to the work I'm doing. She'll be with us through April and will then head off to her next internship as she continues her work towards her MA. I'll be sad to see her go and hope you have all been able to benefit from her time with us. I do hope that starting next fall we'll have another intern, but that will depend on the students' interests. You'll notice a shift in projects for April at those sites we go to once a week in order to work through the process of Genevieve leaving for both her and the residents.

With the number of jobs increasing here are some things to keep in mind:

~ Invoices go out to you by the 5th of the month following the work being done (with 19 places I need to have only one date).

~ On the invoices are the dates I was at your site, so please review to make sure everything matches up, and if there is ever a problem, please call right away.

~ Most of you have scheduled for the entire year on set days (e.g. 1st and 3rd Mondays of the month at 11 a.m.) and I greatly appreciate that. For those who have not scheduled in this way, please realize that those times are locked in, so we will have to schedule your groups around those regularly occurring times. I am giving priority in scheduling to those who schedule for the entire year because it helps all involved with scheduling, reliability, and consistency.

~ Staff members are more than welcome to join any groups and work with residents during art therapy, but please don't work directly on residents' artwork. We are happy to supply enough materials for staff to participate creating their own art. Because I keep notes and digital photos for therapeutic purposes, I need to know what residents are doing on their own. I really appreciate your participation and enthusiasm, so please keep joining us!

Again, thank you for all your trust and support. I am truly enjoying all the time I spend with your elders. Please let me know if there is anything I can do for you and have a wonderful February!

Emery Mikel, MA
Art Therapist
Phone number
emery.mikel@gmail.com

Notes template

This is a sample of what can be used to plan out goals, keep track of attendance, and make brief notes that will later be turned into more complete notes and treatment plans. When doing multiple groups in a day this will help keep groups separate and act as a reminder. Having the first page of the month with the attendance on the top is helpful and then use pages with no attendance and just the other information for the rest of the month's sessions.

Facility: .... **Page #:** ....

	Name													

Date: .... **Intervention:** ....
....

Expectations:
❏ .... Notes ....
....
❏ .... Notes ....
....

Reminiscing ....
Other ....
....

Date: .... **Intervention:** ....
....

Expectations:
❏ .... Notes ....
....
❏ .... Notes ....
....

Reminiscing ....
Other ....
....

SOAP notes sample

SOAP Notes

Week No.: 1   **Date:**

Name: Lily   **Age:**

Context: Initial meeting

Theme/directive: Let's paint a picture. (I will paint as well if she is hesitant because her daughter said she enjoys teaching.)

Media: Watercolor

Goals and objectives: Meet Lily. (Spend a minimum of 20 minutes with her and offer painting materials.)

Subjective: Lily repeatedly refused art materials and seemed to get frustrated, but kept saying the painting I was doing of a tree needed more depth. "It needs more depth." She said, "No" whenever I offered her the brush or asked if she wanted to paint. Then she appeared to give in and after a deep breath took the brush from me. She was silent while working and after creating the depth in the picture herself. However, this may be a sign of acceptance or relaxation based on the slow release of tension from her body and smooth brushstrokes.

Objective: Her body was hunched over in her wheelchair from the beginning and as the session went on her voice grew louder and clearer. She began sighing when I couldn't create the depth she wanted. Her eyes were alert and watched every move I made. About 15 minutes into the the 20 minute session she took the brush from me and created more depth in the tree by combining brown and purple to use on the shadowy side of the tree.

Assessment: She seemed happier when she could take the brush and do the work herself after I had started the painting. Her words come slowly for her, so speaking in short sentences kept some frustration down, but when I couldn't achieve the look she desired she appeared satisfied by taking action. I don't think this was a negative thing in any way. It is something to keep in mind while working with her in future sessions.

Plan: Lily was an artist, so I'd like to try some other materials and see what reactions there are. She seems content with watercolors, but that's also the only thing she has been offered. I want to offer something else after finding out more about her artistic history. Next time: Lily will choose one of two art materials offered.

Bias: Nerves because of first meeting.

Signature .... Date ....

As regulations vary and are ever changing, make sure to research current guidelines for information required on forms.

DAP notes sample

DAP Notes

Week No.: 7   **Date:**
Client Name: Lily   **Age:** 90 years old
Context: First assessment
Theme/directive: Assessment instructions and name of assessment
Media: list specific materials used including type, size, and brand if appropriate
Goals and objectives: Complete [name of assessment] during one .... min. session.

Description: I had asked Lily if she would be willing to do the assessment several days ago and she was very enthusiastic. She showed the same enthusiasm when I asked today. Her eyes opened wider as she smiled, her voice was loud, and she sat up really straight in her wheelchair. She was smiling while I put out everything and watched me closly. Lily didn't ask many questions and worked for 30 minutes, an appropriate amount of time for this assessment, before saying she was done. The first two minutes she just kept repeating the directions. Then she drew. At the end she wrote words at the bottom and said "My Shadow."

Assessment: Lily worked longer then she ever has before when making art with a specific directive. She spent a half hour drawing and didn't appear to become frustrated at any point. Physically she seemed relaxed and her eyes remained focued on her art the entire time she worked. Along with some longer lines there are many details and small marks. All seem intentional and done with control. The paper is over 75 percent covered. She only used the black marker. When she stopped she smiled and seemed pleased with what she had accomplished.

Plan: Evaluate the assessment appropriately (use whatever the correct tools are for rating or evaluating) and reassess in 6 weeks. Then compare the two in order to see changes, similarities, and differences. Administer several other art assessments in order to get a more well-rounded view of Lily and her art.

Bias: I wanted to say more then the assessment allowed, so had to stop from saying too much. I did take the markers out of the box and offer to take the caps off because of prior knowledge of this being a possible difficulty.

Signature .... Date ....

As regulations vary and are ever changing, make sure to research current guidelines for information required on forms.

Treatment plan sample

Lily (Client Name)

Axis I   290.21 Dementia with depressed mood, with behavioral disturbances
Axis II   V 71.09
Axis III   diabetes, urinary tract infections, hypertension, hyperthyroidism, heart murmur, gastroesophegeal reflux
Axis IV   move from home, physical limitations, pain
Axis V   50 (in the past year the highest has been 55)

Complaints:
1. Lily has chronic pain. Making art for too long causes her back and/or arms to hurt.
2. She gets frustrated when she can't verbalize what she's thinking, either from her speech being slow or forgetting a word.
3. Some staff don't listen or cut her off because she speaks slowly. They also patronize her.

Strengths:
1. Lily has an artistic background and continues to enjoy art making.
2. She can make decisions on her own.
3. Her mind is faster than her speech and she understands almost everything said to her.
4. Family ties are strong and her daughter is supportive and visits often.
5. Lily fights for what she wants to the point of yelling or getting physical if her needs are not met.

Short-term goals:
1) Within the next 6 weeks Lily will spend at least 10 minutes each on 3 different assessments.
   Possible Interventions:
   − DDS
   − Face Stimulus Drawings
   − House-Tree-Person
   − PPAT/FEATS.
2) Lily will choose between two different mediums during unstructured art time.
   Interventions:
   − Therapist will offer chalk and oil pastels.
   − Therapist will offer watercolors and acrylic paints.
   − Colored pencils will be added as a third choice when appropriate.
3) Lily will look at her art and discuss it with therapist for five minutes. Single words and short phrases are acceptable.
   Interventions
   − Therapist will bring out old art and lay it on the table for Lily to look over and discuss.
   − Therapist will ask questions that are open ended about pieces.

Long-term goal:
Lily will converse with therapist for at least 10 minutes about a topic of her choosing during structured or unstructured time and make art for at least 15 minutes on the same day.

Signature .... Date ....

(Also remember to date when the goals are met and to update on a regular basis.)

As regulations vary and are ever changing make sure to research current guidelines for information required on forms.

Letter to family

Emery Mikel, MA, ATR-BC, LCAT
Art Therapist
emery.mikel@gmail.com
www.creativelyhealing.com
(Phone number)

Dear Families,

I hope this letter finds everyone enjoying the summer weather! I wanted to take a moment to introduce myself and tell you a little about art therapy and what I do with your family members. In January of 2008, I saw a need for art in many of the retirement homes and communities I visited, so decided I could offer my services to more people as an independent contractor.

My grandmother had Alzheimer's for the last five years of her life and I spent many hours with her even after she no longer recognized me. Art became a new way for us to connect and the time spent making art seemed to lighten any anxiety or confusion that came as the Alzheimer's progressed. Through that time with her, she inspired me to go into the field of art therapy and to begin my work with the elderly. In May of 2007, I completed my MA in Transpersonal Counseling Psychology with an emphasis in Art Therapy at Naropa University. Since then I have worked at multiple facilities with many amazing people and I feel extremely lucky to be doing what I love.

A typical art therapy group focuses on how art making itself is therapeutic, while engaging the participants in ways that promote physical, cognitive, and emotional wellbeing. The projects I bring in are individualized for each group and are designed to create a sense of productivity and empowerment. Through music and discussion the hour together becomes a time to socialize and relate to neighbors while engaging in the common endeavor of art making. The participants are artists whether they have picked up a paint brush before or not.

The next page is a release form that permits me to, anonymously and confidentially, share what we are doing with others for educational purposes. This allows me to better discuss my art therapy program with supervisors and colleagues, to gain insight from others in similar fields, to share my experience at conferences, and ultimately makes me a better therapist. I will always present material in a confidential way so that the person's identity is not revealed. I also respect your decision if you choose not to sign the form and will still enjoy working with your family doing art therapy. Thank you for taking the time to look this over and send the form back in the provided envelope.

Most of the facilities I work with have a calendar that shows when I will be there. Please feel free to join us for an art therapy group when you have the time. I would be happy to talk to you about everything I'm doing and answer any questions you might have. I appreciate your time and hope you have a wonderful summer. If I haven't met you in person, I hope to do so soon.

Thank you,

Emery Mikel, MA, ATR-BC, LCAT
Art Therapist

Release form

Emery Mikel, MA, ATR-BC, LCAT
Art Therapist
emery.mikel@gmail.com
www.creativelyhealing.com
(Phone number)

Art Release Form

I give permission to Emery Mikel, Art Therapist, to photograph the artwork of the below stated person for educational purposes (including, but not limited to, supervision, teaching, research, professional presentation, and/or publications). I further give permission for Emery to share relevant information about the client, medical history, background, and anything pertinent as long as identifying details are changed and confidentiality is protected. I understand that Emery will do everything within her power to make sure this artwork and any information related to it will be kept anonymous and confidential. I further understand that I can contact Emery Mikel at any time to ask questions or change the status of my permission and that my decision will in no way affect the client's treatment.

....
Signature   Date

....
Print name   Relationship to client

Permission given for ....

Client's place of residence ....

Comments or questions:

....
....
....
....
....

As regulations vary and are ever changing, make sure to research current guidelines for information required on forms.

Release form II

Emery Mikel, MA, ATR-BC, LCAT
Art Therapist
emery.mikel@gmail.com
www.creativelyhealing.com
(Phone number)

Informed Consent

Client's name   ....
Facility name   ....
Therapist's name   ....

I give permission for the display of my artwork in conjunction with my treatment:

❑ within the facility
❑ outside of the facility.

I give consent to my therapist to use my artwork for educational or research purposes (including, but not limited to, supervision, teaching, research, professional presentation, and/or publication):

❑ within the facility
❑ outside of the facility.

I understand that I have the right to revoke this authorization at any time. I am aware that if I revoke or refuse to sign this authorization it will not affect my treatment.

Patient's signature ....
Date ....

❑ I certify that I have received a copy of this release form.

Therapist's signature ....
Date ....

When appropriate make space for intern and supervisor signature or the client's power of attorney.

As regulations vary and are ever changing, make sure to research current guidelines for information required on forms.

Intern release form

The Intern agrees to:
- maintain confidentiality at all times
- change the name and other facts about the resident when discussing residents outside of Internship
- follow ethical principles as laid out by the facility, American Psychological Association, American Art Therapy Association, and any other set of guidelines that apply
- protect and securely store client artwork in the art studio when it is not kept in the resident's own room.

Client or Guardian agrees that the intern can:
- talk about the resident and art made by the resident with facility staff and supervisor
- talk about the resident and art made by the resident in class with peers and the instructors
- talk about the resident and art made by the resident with the instructors privately
- talk about the resident and art made by the resident with her private therapist
- take and show art to staff at internship, supervisor, peers, and instructors in the situations described above
- discuss or write about the resident and art made by the resident in education situations and professional situations after graduation (including, but not limited to, conferences, articles for professional journals, and case presentations)
- photograph the art, so the originals remain with the resident.

Artwork:
(Please check all that apply)
- ❑ can be displayed with artist's name at facility
- ❑ can be displayed anonymously at facility
- ❑ can be photographed by intern and kept with resident's file
- ❑ can be photographed by intern for use by intern at Internship or in school (example: when the original is not available or is on display somewhere)
- ❑ can be photographed by intern for use after graduation for educational or professional purposes as stated above.

By signing below all three parties have read and agree to the above statements. All three parties understand that the resident or guardian has the ability to change, amend, or cancel the agreement at any time by notifying the intern or her supervisor. In any situation confidentiality will be upheld by the intern and her supervisor and will not affect the care or treatment of the resident.

For anything outside of the above situations the intern will obtain written permission prior to the situation occuring.

....
Resident or guardian signature   Print name   Date

....
Intern signature   Print name   Date

....

Supervisor signature   Print name   Date

As regulations vary and are ever changing make sure to research current guidelines for information required on forms.

PROJECTS

For more descriptions and images of projects, please visit www.creativelyhealing.com.

Quilts

Skills developed and utilized

- Dexterity and coordination to hold down fabric while drawing.
- Manipulation of scissors to cut fabric.
- Planning and imagination in creating an image with layers of fabric and markers.
- Sensory stimulation from fabric.
- Reminiscence about the topic, quilts, quilting, fabric, family life, and chores.

Materials

- A fabric base (muslin, white, or light cotton material).
- Pre-cut pieces that fit a theme (keep it simple: circles, ovals, strips—see themes on pp. 181–2).
- Small pieces of fabric that participants can cut up.
- Scissors.
- Fabric or tacky glue.
- Fabric markers.
- Table cloth.
- Smock/protection from fabric markers.

Steps

1. Hand out fabric base (can be pre-glued to a larger colored piece of fabric to form a border).

2. Explain topic (i.e. trees, flowers, light and dark, water, landscape) and pass out pre-cut fabric.

3. Place scissors and other fabric on the table with glue.

4. Offer fabric markers as an alternative to cutting/gluing or as a way to embellish pre-cut fabric pieces.

5. Title and sign.

Modifications/variations

- This project can be done in a single session or over several sessions,

- The group can make one large image (36 × 48 inches) or each person can create a smaller quilt block (e.g. 6 × 6, 12 × 12, 6 × 12 inches).

- Smaller pieces can be combined into a larger quilt later. When this is the case, a theme (e.g. seasons) might be used to tie the patches together.

- High-functioning—More cutting and creating on the participants' part. Give more colors and options and discuss themes that can be used. One goal is for them to create a cohesive image with multiple colors and pieces either on their own or with the rest of the group.

- Mid-functioning—Have choices available. Aim for an image without as much focus on reality or color. More abstract themes (the colors of spring) can allow for more creativity if focusing on something specific becomes difficult or there are memory issues.

- Low-functioning—Emphasis on arranging pre-cut pieces and drawing. Talking about themes or images will add to conversation. Allow it to end up in whatever way the participants are able to arrange it. The markers may end up arranged on the fabric as if they were a part of the collage. When it's time to pick them up, make a line the length and color of the marker where it was sitting to keep the intent as a part of the patch. Be ready to volunteer to glue pieces down.

Notes/observations

Having the fabric base pre-cut and glued to a slightly larger colorful piece of fabric helps give the participants a starting place. If too much is set out on the table at once or things are disorganized, confusion is likely to occur. Keeping things organized by color and in small amounts is imperative for the lower-functioning groups. Markers can be used for those who are unsure about the fabric, especially if they are more used to drawing or painting. If participants live at the facility, making a quilt that can hang on a wall is a great way to show the group's productivity to the community. It can give participants the feeling that they contributed to something bigger than themselves. The key is to start small and let it grow naturally. If everyone makes a small square the first time, you can always go bigger next time or create several small squares to make a larger wall hanging. Make it possible to adjust as the participants give feedback about what they are comfortable with.

Themes

Spring

Using bright colors, and cut out shapes to make the following:

- flowers (petal shapes, stems, small leaf shapes)
- trees (strips of brown, green scraps for leaves, circles for apples)
- sun (yellow circles, strips for rays)
- birds (a V shape can be a bird flying in the distance)
- clouds (white circles or ovals; cotton balls are fun too!).

Self-portraits

- Have each person create their face out of material.
- Connect each portrait together to make a quilt.
- Make individual pillows that clients can take home.

- This could be all fabric or some drawing.

Patterns

- Lines of color.
- Swirls.
- Start on the outside to create a border and work your way in using shapes and colors.
- Start in the center and create concentric rings of colors.
- Use pre-cut squares to cover the base fabric.

Mosaics

If you are unsure about what will end up in people's mouths, just use beans the first time! Still be wary about the choking hazards.

Skills developed and utilized

- Manipulation of tiles, rocks, and other materials of various shapes and sizes.
- Sorting objects of similar size and color.
- Use of fine motor skills to pick up and manipulate small objects.
- Hand–eye coordination, choosing a small piece that fits in the open space in the mosaic.
- Negotiation and communication around need for certain colors and help with arranging.
- Flexibility when there aren't enough of a specific color or material.

Materials

- Tiles, rocks, glass beads, beans, and other objects suitable for mosaics.

- Tacky or mosaic glue (helps if it's stronger than white Elmer's [or other all-purpose] glue). Don't be skimpy, but always look for non-toxic!

- A base—foamcore or balsa wood (size and shape dependent on participants' needs/abilities).

- Popsicle sticks for pushing objects around or applying glue.

- Marker or pencil if you want to predraw images on the work surface.

- I do not suggest using grout—in fact, I advise against it. If you decide to use it, please follow safety precautions. Some brands are toxic or can cause respiratory issues.

Project

Option A:

- Apply glue to entire work surface.
- Place pieces on glue and press down.

Option B:

- Glue one piece at a time.

Option C:

- Lay out design first.
- Glue from one side to the other or from center out.

In any of these options, the design can be abstract or realistic. Some people will lay out patterns or use colors they like, while others design a picture such as a tree using pinto beans and green split peas.

Modifications

- To do this over several sessions, use a larger work surface and split up the project into sections (i.e. lay out then glue, or work on various sections each session). Another choice is to work with multiple bases and focus on building skills over sessions, from getting used to the materials to laying out a pattern or specific image.

- High-functioning—Individuals can use many different materials that are of varying sizes. Patterns and images should be explored and expected. Make sure to have enough of several colors in order to allow several people to create the patterns and images they want.

- Mid-functioning—The first time use beans to make sure everyone understands the materials and doesn't try to eat them. Then offer some guidelines and examples for patterns and images.

- Low-functioning—Use beans to start with until oral fixations are known. Each group is different and it helps to have assistants when first trying this. An option where everyone helps the art therapist make one large mosaic for the facility can benefit everyone while setting boundaries on who does what and offering a little more control to the therapist.

Notes/observations

Beans are a good way to start in order to find out how the participants will handle the project without as much danger in case they try to eat the pieces. Having examples can help start people off although high-functioning individuals will usually start on their own. If the materials are laid out and then glued down, it's easiest to push everything over a quarter inch, put a line of glue down, and shift one line at a time back onto the glue.

Themes
Trees

- Use brown colored beans to create the trunk.
- Green split peas can be grass and leaves.
- A black bean can be a bird.
- Yellow split peas make up the sun.
- Fill in the background with white beans as filler.

Patterns

- Begin in the center and then use other colored beans to build outward in a spiral or as a burst.

- Lines of colored beans.

- Start with a border and then create a pattern inside.

- Use black and white beans to create a repetitive pattern.

RESOURCES AND READING SUGGESTIONS

I have compiled some of my favorite books and information here. While it is by no means a complete list, I hope something below will inspire you in some way. There are categories to help as you look through the lists, but keep in mind that every book helped me with my self-employment and contract work in some way, regardless of the topic. I mainly included information I am familiar with and, because I am only one person, this might mean you have some wonderful books, articles, or websites you have found in your journey that I have not discovered yet. Please share your suggestions with others and let me know if there is something I just have to read or that made you excited about your work. Enjoy the suggestions below!

P.S. My favorite list is "Other interesting books"!

Self-employment and small business

- California Employment Development Department (EDD)— www.edd.ca.gov/Disability/Self-Employed.htm.

- Freelancers Union—www.freelancersunion.org.

- The US Small Business Administration—www.sba.gov.

Many states have their own small business development centers or organizations to help out those starting a business, so make sure to check out your local resources.

Books

Carroll, M. (2007) *The Mindful Leader: Awakening Your Natural Management Skills Through Mindfulness Meditation.* Boston, MA: Trumpeter.
Fishman, S. (2011) *Working for Yourself: Law and Taxes for Independent Contractors, Freelancers and Consultants* (8th edition). California: NOLO.

Gilman, C. (1997) *Doing Work You Love: Discovering Your Purpose and Realizing Your Dreams*. New York, NY: Barnes & Noble Books.
Godin, S. (2011) *Lynchpin: Are You Indispensable?* New York, NY: Portfolio Trade.
McMeekin, G. (2011) *The 12 Secrets of Highly Successful Women: A Portable Life Coach for Creative Women*. San Francisco, CA: Conari Press.
Mycoskie, B. (2011) *Start Something That Matters*. New York, NY: Spiegel & Grau.
Sivers, D. (2011) *Anything You Want: 40 Lessons for a New Kind of Entrepreneur*. USA: The Domino Project.

Look for books written by others who have started their own business in a creative way. There are also many blogs out there that you might find interesting. Seth Godin's is one of my favorites and very inspiring!

Creative arts therapy

- American Music Therapy Association (AMTA)—www.musictherapy.org.
  - Great Lakes Region—www.glr-amta.org.
  - Mid-Atlantic Region—www.mar-amta.org.
  - New England Region—www.musictherapynewengland.org.
  - Southeastern Region—www.ser-amta.org.
  - Southwestern Region—www.swamta.com.
  - Midwest Region—www.und.nodak.edu/org/amtamidwestern/Welcome.html.
  - Western Region—www.wramta.org.
- Art Therapy Alliance—www.arttherapyalliance.org.
- International Expressive Arts Therapy Association (IEATA)—www.ieata.org.
- Music Therapy Ed—www.musictherapyed.com.
- World Federation of Music Therapy (WFMT)—www.musictherapyworld.net.

There are many more!

Books

Gantt, L. and Tabone, C. (1998) *The Formal Elements Art Therapy Scale: The Rating Manual.* Morgantown, WV: Gargoyle Press.

Gantt, L. and Tabone, C. (2003) "The Formal Elements Art Therapy Scale and 'Draw a Person Picking an Apple from a Tree.'" In C. Malchiodi (ed.) *Handbook of Art Therapy.* New York, NY: Guilford Press.

Garai, J. (2001) "Humanistic Art Therapy." In J. Rubin (ed.) *Approaches to Art Therapy: Theory and Technique.* New York, NY: Brunner-Routledge.

Hass-Cohen, N. and Carr, R. (eds) (2008) *Art Therapy and Clinical Neuroscience.* London: Jessica Kingsley Publishers.

Kramer, E. (2000) *Art as Therapy: Collected Papers* (edited by L.A. Gerity). London: Jessica Kingsley Publishers.

McNiff, S. (1992) *Art as Medicine: Creating a Therapy of the Imagination.* Boston, MA: Shambhala.

Malchiodi, C. (2002) *The Soul's Palette: Drawing on Art's Transformative Powers for Health and Well-being.* Boston, MA: Shambhala.

Malchiodi, C. (ed.) (2003) *Handbook of Art Therapy.* New York, NY: Guilford Press.

Moon, B. (2010) *Art-based Group Therapy: Theory and Practice.* Springfield, IL: Charles C. Thomas.

Moon, C.H. (2002) *Studio Art Therapy: Cultivating the Artist Identity in the Art Therapist.* London: Jessica Kingsley Publishers.

Rubin, J. (ed.) (2001) *Approaches to Art Therapy: Theory and Technique.* New York, NY: Brunner-Routledge.

Assessments

PPAT—Gantt, L., and Tabone, C. (1998) *The Formal Elements Art Therapy Scale: The rating manual.* Morgantown, WV: Gargoyle Press.

DDS—Cohen, B.M. (1985) *The diagnostic drawing series handbook* (available from Barry M. Cohen, P.O. Box 9853, Alexandria, Virginia, USA 22304).

KHTP—Burns, R. C. (1987) *Kinetic-house-tree-person drawings (K-H-T-P): An interpretative manual.* New York : Brunner/Mazel

Bridge Drawing—Hays, R., & Lyons, S. (1981) "The bridge drawing: A projective technique for assessment in art therapy." *The Arts in Psychotherapy, 8,* 207-217.

Bird's Nest—Kaiser, D. (2009) "Assessing attachment with the bird's nest drawing: A review of the research." *Art Therapy: Journal of the American Art Therapy Association 26,* 1, 26-33.

Transpersonal and Buddhism

- Shambhala—www.shambhala.org.

- Naropa University—www.naropa.edu.

Books

Chogyam Trungpa (1984) *Shambhala: The Sacred Path of the Warrior* (edited by C.R. Gimian). Boston, MA: Shambhala.

Cortright, B. (1997) *Psychotherapy and Spirit: Theory and Practice in Transpersonal Psychotherapy.* Albany, NY: State University of New York Press.

Dalai Lama (2006) *How to See Yourself as You Really Are* (edited and translated by J. Hopkins). New York, NY: Atria Books.

Hayward, J. and Hayward, K. (1998) *Sacred World: The Shambhala Way to Gentleness, Bravery, and Power* (2nd edition). Boston, MA: Shambhala.

Kabat-Zinn, A. (2005) *Wherever You Go, There You Are.* New York, NY: Hyperion.

McLeod, M. (ed.) (2011) *Your True Home: The Everyday Wisdom of Thich Nhat Hanh*. Boston, MA: Shambhala.

Walsh, R. (2000) *Essential Spirituality: The Seven Central Practices to Awaken Heart and Mind*. New York, NY: Wiley.

Watkins, M. (1996) *Waking Dreams* (3rd edition). Woodstock, CT: Spring Publications.

Seniors and Alzheimer's

- Alzheimer's Association—www.alz.org.

- Alzheimer's Foundation of America—www.alzfdn.org.

Books

Abraham, R. (2005) *When Words Have Lost Their Meaning: Alzheimer's Patients Communicate Through Art*. Westport, CT: Praeger.

Bracker, J. (2003) *Creating Moments of Joy*. West Lafayette, IN: Purdue University Press.

Cohen, G.D. (2000) *The Creative Age: Awakening Human Potential in the Second Half of Life*. New York, NY: HarperCollins.

DeBaggio, T. (2003) *Losing My Mind: An Intimate Look at Life with Alzheimer's*. New York, NY: The Free Press.

Driscoll, E. (2004) *Alzheimer's: A Handbook for the Caretaker*. Boston, MA: Branden Books.

Galbraith, A., Subrin, R., and Ross, D. (2008) "Alzheimer's Disease: Art, Creativity and the Brain." In N. Hass-Cohen and R. Carr (eds) *Art Therapy and Clinical Neuroscience*. London: Jessica Kingsley Publishers.

Hayes, J. and Povey, S. (2011) *The Creative Arts in Dementia Care: Practical Person-Centred Approaches and Ideas*. London: Jessica Kingsley Publishers.

Kubler-Ross, E. (1969) *On Death and Dying: What the Dying Have to Teach Doctors, Nurses, Clergy, and Their Own Families*. New York, NY: Macmillan.

Peterson, B. (2004) *Voices of Alzheimer's: Courage, Humor, Hope, and Love in the Face of Dementia*. Cambridge, MA: De Capo Press.

Schachter-Shalomi, Z. and Miller, R.S. (1997) *From Age-ing to Sage-ing: A Profound New Vision of Growing Older*. New York, NY: Grand Central Publishing.

Simpson, A. and Simpson, R. (1999) *Through the Wilderness of Alzheimer's: A Guide in Two Voices*. Minneapolis, MN: Augsburg Fortress Publishers.

Snowdown, D. (2001) *Aging with Grace: What the Nun Study Teaches Us about Leading Longer, Healthier, and More Meaningful Lives*. New York, NY: Bantum Books.

Thomas, W.H. (2004) *What Are Old People For?* St. Louis, MO: VanderWyk & Burnham.

Other interesting books

Adams, P. and Mylander, M. (1998) *Gesundheit! Bringing Good Health to You, the Medical System, and Society through Physician Service, Complementary Therapies, Humor, and Joy*. Rochester, VT: Healing Arts Press.

Allen, R.F. and Allen, S.D. (1995) *Winnie-the-Pooh on Problem Solving: In Which Pooh, Piglet, and Friends Explore How to Solve Problems So You Can Too*. New York, NY: Dutton.

Bloomfield, H., Colgrove, M., and McWilliams, P. (2000) *How to Survive the Loss of a Love*. Algonac, MI: Mary Books/Prelude Press.

Gerber, R. (2003) *Leadership the Eleanor Roosevelt Way: Timeless Strategies from the First Lady of Courage*. New York, NY: Portfolio.

Hsu, A. (1997) *The Sword Polisher's Record: The Way of Kung Fu*. Tokyo: Tuttle Publishing.

Kimball, K. (2010) *The Dirty Life: On Farming, Food, and Love.* New York, NY: Scribner.
Marinelli, D. (2010) *The Comet and the Tornado.* New York, NY: Sterling.
Pausch, R. and Zaslow, J. (2008) *The Last Lecture.* New York, NY: Hyperion.
Powell, C. and Koltz, T. (2012) *It Worked for Me: In Life and Leadership.* New York, NY: HarperCollins.
Reynolds, P. (2003) *The Dot.* Cambridge, MA: Candlewick Press.
Reynolds, P. (2004) *Ish.* Cambridge, MA: Candlewick Press.
Sacks, O. (1996) *An Anthropologist on Mars: Seven Paradoxical Tales.* New York, NY: Vintage Books.
Sacks, O. (1998) *The Man Who Mistook His Wife for a Hat and Other Clinical Tales.* New York, NY: Touchstone.
Sacks, O. (2007) *Musicophilia: Tales of Music and the Brain.* Canada: Knopf.
Siegel, D. (2010) *The Mindful Therapist: A Clinician's Guide to Mindsight and Neural Integration.* New York, NY: W.W. Norton & Company.
Sun Tzu. (1963) *The Art of War* (translated by S.B. Griffith). London: Oxford University Press.
Taylor, J. (2009) *My Stroke of Insight: A Brain Scientist's Personal Journey.* New York, NY: Viking.
Thubron, C. (2012) *To a Mountain in Tibet.* New York, NY: Harper Perennial.

Organizations, ethics, and credentialing

- American Art Therapy Association (AATA)—www.arttherapy.org/aata-ethics.html.
- American Counseling Association—www.counseling.org/resources/codeofethics/TP/home/ct2.aspx.
- American Dance Therapy Association (ADTA)—www.adta.org/resources/Documents/CODE_of_ethics1.pdf.
- American Music Therapy Association (AMTA)—www.musictherapy.org/about/ethics.
- American Psychological Association (APA)—www.apa.org/ethics/code/index.aspx.
- Art Therapy Credentials Board (ATCB)—www.atcb.org/code_of_professional_practice.
- Certification Board for Music Therapists (CBMT)—www.cbmt.org.
- Health Insurance Portability and Accountability Act (HIPAA) Guidelines—www.hhs.gov/ocr/privacy/index.html.
- International Expressive Arts Therapy Association (IEATA)—www.ieata.org/reat-ethics.html.
- National Association for Drama Therapy (NADT)—www.nadt.org.
- NY State Office of Professions, Mental Health Practitioners—www.op.nysed.gov/prof/mhp.

Books

Dileo, C. (2000) *Ethical thinking in music therapy.* Cherry Hill, NJ: Jeffrey Books

Furman, L.R. (2013). *Ethics in art therapy: Challenging topics for a complex modality.* London: Jessica Kingsley Publishers.

Moon, B. (2006) *Ethical issues in art therapy.* Springfield, IL: Charles C. Thomas Publisher.

Taylor, K. (1995) *Ethics of caring: Honoring the web of life in our professional healing relationships.* Santa Cruz, CA: Hanford Mead Publishers, Inc.

Have fun finding your local, national, and international organizations. These are great resources and a way to connect with new friends and colleagues who can inspire, mentor, or support you in your endeavors. Create a community for yourself and others by connecting with people all around the world. Share your knowledge and learn from theirs.

Articles

Allen, P.B. (2008) "Commentary on community-based art studios: Underlying principles." *Art Therapy: Journal of the American Art Therapy Association 25,* 1, 11–12.

Callanan, B.O. (2004) "Art therapy with the frail elderly." *Journal of Long Term Home Health Care 13,* 2, 20–23.

Carroll, L. (2006) "The art of therapy." *Neurology Now 2,* 6, 24–7.

Chaudhury, H. (2003) "Remembering home through art." *Alzheimer's Care Quarterly 4,* 2, 119–24.

Chinen, A.B. (1985) "Fairy tales and transpersonal development in later life." *The Journal of Transpersonal Psychology 17,* 2.

Cohen, B.M. (1985) "The diagnostic drawing series handbook." (Available from Barry M. Cohen, P.O. Box 9853, Alexandria, Virginia, USA 22304.)

Cohen, B.M. (1986/1994) "The diagnostic drawing series rating guide." (Available from Barry M. Cohen, P.O. Box 9853, Alexandria, Virginia, USA 22304.)

Cohen, B.M., Hammer, J., and Singer, S. (1988) "The diagnostic drawing series: A systematic approach to art therapy evaluation and research." *The Arts in Psychotherapy 15,* 11–21.

Cohen, B.M., Mills, A., and Kijak, A. (1994) "An introduction to the diagnostic drawing series: A standardized tool for diagnostic and clinical use." *Art Therapy 11,* 2, 105–10.

Cohen, G.D. (2006) "Research on creativity and aging: The positive impact of the arts on health and illness." *Generations: Journal of the American Society on Aging XXX,* I, 7–15.

Fornazzari, L.R. (1995) "Preserved painting creativity in an artist with Alzheimer's disease." *European Journal of Neurology 12,* 419–24.

Hannemann, B.T. (2006) "Creativity with dementia patients: Can creativity and art stimulate dementia patients positively?" *Gerontology 52,* 59–65.

Harlan, J. (1990) "Beyond the patient to the person: Promoting aspects of the autonomous functioning in individuals with mild to moderate dementia." *American Journal of Art Therapy 28,* 4, 99–105.

Johnston, N. (2004) "Expressions of Alzheimer's." *Alzheimer's Care Quarterly 5,* 4, 278–88.

Jonas-Simpson, C. and Mitchell, G.J. (2005) "Giving voice to expressions of quality of life for persons living with dementia through story, music, and art." *Alzheimer's Care Quarterly 6,* 1, 52–61.

Kamar, O. (1997) "Light and death: Art therapy with a patient with Alzheimer's disease." *American Journal of Art Therapy 35,* 4, 118–25.

Kerr, C.C. (1999) "The psychosocial significance of creativity in the elderly." *Art Therapy 16,* 1, 37–41.

Kinney, J.M. and Rentz, C.A. (2005) "Observed well-being among individuals with dementia: Memories in the making, an art program, versus other structured activity." *American Journal of Alzheimer's Disease and Other Dementias 20,* 4, 220–27.

Kramer, E. (1986) "The art therapist's third hand: Reflections on art, art therapy, and society at large." *American Journal of Art Therapy 24*, 71–86.

Kramer, R. and Iager, A. (1984) "The use of art in assessment of psychotic disorders: Changing perspectives." *The Arts in Psychotherapy 11*, 3, 197–201.

Kuhn, D., Ortigara, A., and Kasayka, R.E. (2000) "Dementia care mapping: An innovative tool to measure person-centered care." *Alzheimer's Care Quarterly 1*, 3, 7–15.

Lau, R. and Cheng, S. (2011) "Gratitude lessens death anxiety." *European Journal of Ageing 8*, 3, 169–75.

Lehmann, H. and Risquez, F. (1953) "The use of finger paintings in the clinical evaluation of psychotic conditions: A quantitative and qualitative approach." *Journal of Mental Science 99*, 763–77.

MacFarlane, J.W. (1942) "Problems of validation inherent in projective methods." *American Journal of Orthopsychiatry 12*, 405–10.

Mills, A., Cohen, B.M., and Meneses, J.Z. (1993) "Reliability and validity tests of the Diagnostic Drawing Series." *The Arts in Psychotherapy 20*, 1, 83–8.

Riley, S. (2004) "The creative mind." *Art Therapy: Journal of the American Art Therapy Association 21*, 4, 184–90.

Safar, L.T. and Press, D.Z. (2011) "Art and the brain: Effects of dementia on art production in art therapy." *Art Therapy: Journal of the American Art Therapy Association 28*, 3, 96–103.

Sifton, C.B. (2002) "Lessons on listening: The art of communication." *Alzheimer's Care Quarterly 3*, 2, iv–vi.

Silver, R. (1993) "Assessing the emotional content of drawings by older adults: Research findings and implications." *American Journal of Art Therapy 32*, 46–52.

Stewart, E. (2004) "Art therapy and neuroscience blend: Working with patients who have dementia." *Art Therapy: Journal of the American Art Therapy Association 21*, 3, 148–55.

Tinnin, L. (1990) "Biological processes in nonverbal communication and their role in the making and interpretation of art." *American Journal of Art Therapy 29*, 1, 9–13.

Ulman, E. and Levy, B. (1967) "Judging psychopathology from paintings." *Journal of Abnormal Psychology 72*, 182–7.

Wald, J. (1983) "Alzheimer's disease and the role of art therapy in its treatment." *American Journal of Art Therapy 22*, 57–64.

Williams, K., Agell, G., Gantt, L., and Goodman, R. (1996) "Art-based diagnosis: Fact or fantasy?" *American Journal of Art Therapy 35*, 9–31.

INDEX